Exploring Motion and Forces

Speed, Acceleration, and Friction

Science Journal

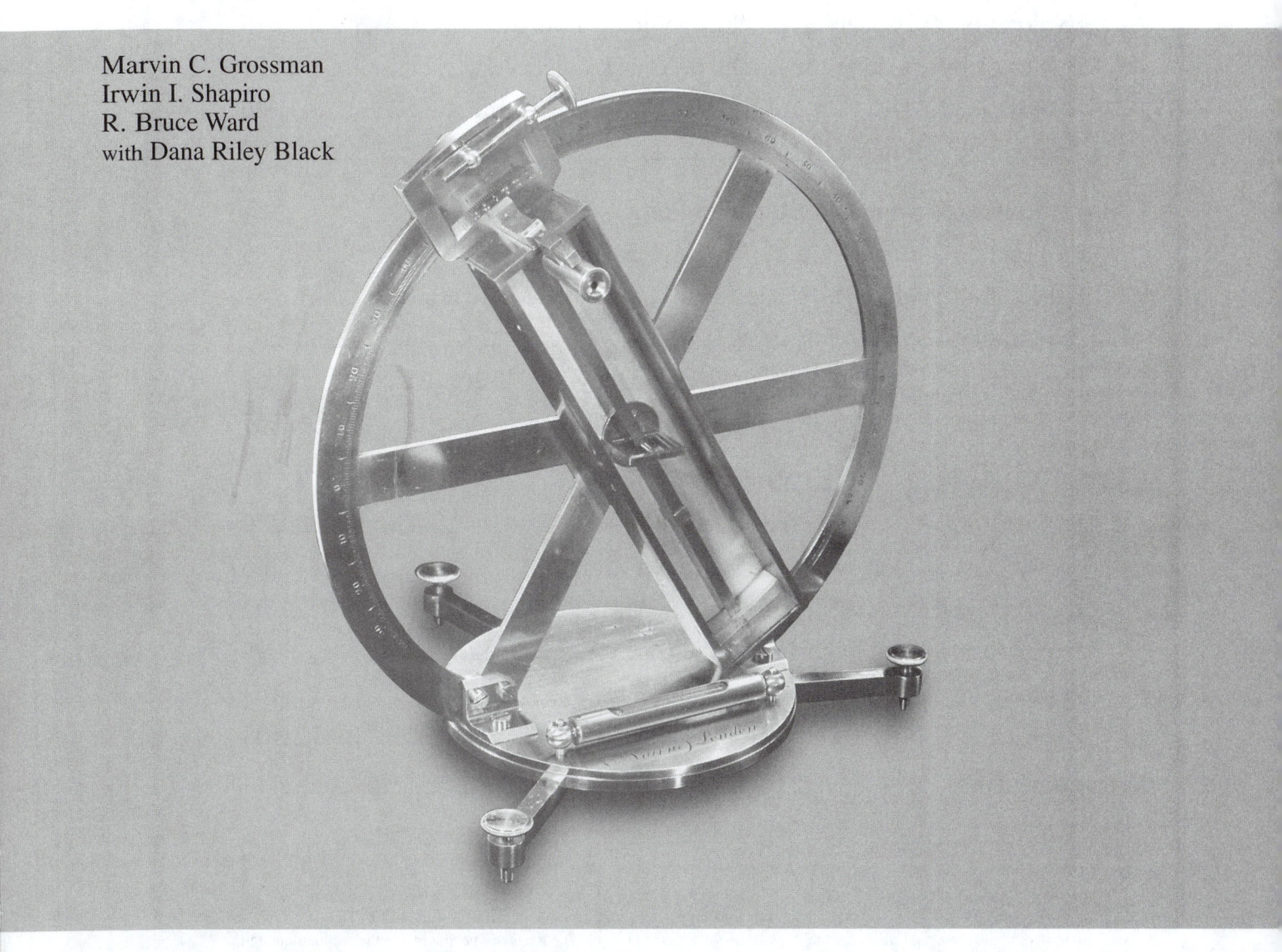

Marvin C. Grossman
Irwin I. Shapiro
R. Bruce Ward
with Dana Riley Black

ARIES: Astronomy-Based Physical Science

Developed at the Harvard-Smithsonian Center for Astrophysics
Supported by the National Science Foundation

Charlesbridge

EXPLORING MOTION AND FORCES — Table of Contents

UNIT 1: Motion All Around
Exploration 1: Motion in Your World 1

Exploration 2: What Makes Things Stop and Go? 5

UNIT 2: The Super Sliding Disk
Exploration 3: Let's Get Moving 10

Exploration 4: Launching the Super Sliding Disk 15

Exploration 5: Testing the Limits of Your Launcher 21

Exploration 6: There's a Lot of Friction in This World 26

Exploration 7: Floating on Air 30

UNIT 3: Rolling Motion on an Inclined Plane
Exploration 8: Setting Up the Track 35

Exploration 9: How Far Does It Roll? 44

Exploration 10: How Fast Does It Roll? 53

Exploration 11: Rolling Speed Along a Horizontal Track 62

Exploration 12: Rolling Speed on an Inclined Track 67

UNIT 4: Acceleration and the ARIES Speedcart
Exploration 13: Building the Speedcart 79

Exploration 14: Powering the Speedcart 86

Exploration 15: Increasing the Falling Mass 92

Exploration 16: Adding Mass to the Cart 98

Exploration 17: A Fan-Powered Speedcart 103

Exploration 18: How Fast Can the Fan Cart Move? 108

Keep on Moving 114

Cover photo courtesy of Harvard University, Collection of Historical Scientific Instruments.

The cover photograph shows a Dip Needle made by Edward Narine of London in 1765. The Dip Needle is used to indicate the angle of the Earth's magnetic lines of force, which do not always follow the surface of the Earth. The vertical brass circle is mounted on a horizontal brass base with a copper level. The magnetic needle inside the rectangular brass box can move because it is mounted on pivots.

Copyright © 2001 President and Fellows of Harvard College.

This material is based upon work supported by the National Science Foundation under Grant Nos. MDR-9154113 and ESI-9553845. Any opinions, findings, and conclusions or recommendations expressed in this material are those of the authors and do not necessarily reflect the views of the National Science Foundation.

CHARLESBRIDGE PUBLISHING, 85 Main Street, Watertown, MA 02472 • www.charlesbridge.com • All rights reserved. No part of this publication may be reproduced, stored in a retrieval system, or transmitted in whole or in part, in any form or by any means (electronic, mechanical, photocopying, recording, or otherwise) without the prior written permission of the Publisher.

ISBN: 1-57091-257-2

Printed in Canada   10 9 8 7 6

Unit 1: MOTION ALL AROUND

Exploration 1: Motion in Your World

RECORDING YOUR IDEAS

1. What do you think is meant by the word *motion*?

2. How can you tell that something is moving?

3. List six things that you have observed moving and describe the movement that took place.

4. Write at least six verbs that can be used to tell how an object moves.

5. Can you think of a way numbers could be used to measure or describe motion?

6. My question about motion is

EXPLORATION 1 PROCEDURE

1. Find a moving object in nature.

    Name of object: _____

    What is your evidence that the object moved?
    _____
    _____

    What words best describe the object's motion?
    _____

    Why do you think the object started moving?
    _____

    If your object is in constant motion, why do you think it keeps moving?
    _____
    _____

2. Find another moving object in nature.

    Name of object: _____

    What is your evidence that the object moved?
    _____
    _____

    What words best describe the object's motion?
    _____

    Why do you think the object started moving?
    _____

    If your object is in constant motion, why do you think it keeps moving?
    _____
    _____

3. Find a moving object in the classroom.

   Name of object: _____

   What is your evidence that the object moved?

   _____

   _____

   What words best describe the object's motion?

   _____

   What do you think made the object start moving?

   _____

   If your object is in constant motion, why do you think it keeps moving?

   _____

   _____

4. Find another moving object in the classroom.

   Name of object: _____

   What is your evidence that the object moved?

   _____

   _____

   What words best describe the object's motion?

   _____

   What do you think made the object start moving?

   _____

   If your object is in constant motion, why do you think it keeps moving?

   _____

   _____

INTERPRETING THE RESULTS

? **1.** Some objects, such as a leaf, a roll of masking tape, or a pencil, move in different ways. Describe what those motions could be and what might cause these objects to move.

_____

_____

_____

? **2.** How do you know when something is moving? What evidence do you look for?

_____

_____

? **3.** Describe the motion of an object that is thrown up into the air.

_____

_____

? **4.** In what ways are the motions of objects you observed outside your classroom similar to the motions of objects you observed in your classroom?

_____

_____

_____

What I know about the motion of objects

_____

_____

_____

_____

_____

Exploration 2: What Makes Things Stop and Go?

RECORDING YOUR IDEAS

? 1. Look at the ball on the table. Is it possible for the ball to start moving by itself? What evidence do you have for your answer?

_____
_____
_____

? 2. Is it possible for any object to start moving by itself? What evidence do you have for your answer?

_____
_____
_____

? 3. If you pushed the ball to start it moving, how would the strength of the push affect the motion?

_____
_____
_____

? 4. Once the ball starts moving, will it keep moving forever? If not, what might cause it to stop?

_____
_____
_____

? 5. My question about moving things is

_____
_____
_____

EXPLORATION 2 PROCEDURE

Part 1: Applying a Force

1. With a partner, find an object that can be easily moved across a horizontal surface.

2. Start the object in motion by applying the least push necessary to get it moving.

3. Describe the motion after you stopped applying the push.

   _____
   _____

4. Apply a slightly larger push. Describe the motion after you stop the push.

   _____
   _____

5. How does this motion compare with the motion that resulted when you used a smaller push?

   _____
   _____

Part 2: This Vehicle Makes Sudden Stops

Collect the following materials with your partner.

✔	Materials Checklist
	A small, flat object, such as an eraser or 15 centimeter (about 6 inch) ruler
	2 hardbound books of about the same thickness
	Metric ruler

1. Place the small object on the cover of one of the books.

2. Move the book across the desk as fast as you can without making the object change its position on the book.

3. Place the second book on your desk and hold it in place with one hand. This is the barrier.

4. Place the book with the object 15 centimeters (about 6 inches) away from the barrier book. Move the book with the object at about the same speed as you did before, but this time make it hit the barrier.

5. Describe the motion of the object when it is on the moving book.

6. What happens after the book stops moving?

7. Does this experiment remind you of a situation you have been in yourself? If so, describe it.

Part 3: Throwing a Coin

For this part of the exploration, you will need a coin.

1. Throw the coin up in the air and observe its motion.

2. How did you get the coin to move upward?

3. What might affect how high the coin went?

4. Why do you think the coin came back down?
   _____
   _____

5. Place the coin on your desk and give it a push. Describe the motion.
   _____
   _____

6. Why do you think the coin stopped moving?
   _____
   _____

7. How is the motion of a coin thrown into the air similar to the motion of a coin moving on a horizontal surface?
   _____
   _____
   _____

8. What do you think affects how far you can throw a coin when you throw it in a horizontal direction?
   _____
   _____
   _____

9. If no one caught the coin, what would happen to it?
   _____
   _____
   _____

INTERPRETING THE RESULTS

1. Is there a relationship between how hard you push an object in a horizontal direction and how far it moves? If so, describe the relationship.

_____

_____

2. While an object is in motion, why do you think it keeps going?

_____

_____

3. Describe the motion of an object from the instant that it is thrown up into the air until it returns to the ground.

_____

_____

_____

4. Was there a difference between the motion of the object placed on the sliding book and the motion of the book itself? If so, describe the difference.

_____

_____

_____

What I know about forces (pushes or pulls) and motion

_____

_____

_____

_____

Unit 2: THE SUPER SLIDING DISK

Exploration 3: Let's Get Moving

RECORDING YOUR IDEAS

1. Put a small object on the floor and give it a push with your hand. Describe the object's motion.

2. If you put the same object on a frozen lake and gave it a push, how would the motion be different from its motion on the floor?

3. Why do you think so?

4. Is the distance the object moves affected by how hard you initially push it? If so, in what way is it affected?

5. Why do you think you need to wear a seat belt when riding in a car?

6. My question about forces (pushes and pulls) and motion is

EXPLORATION 3 PROCEDURE

✔	**Materials Checklist**
	12 centimeter x 12 centimeter (4 ¾ inch x 4 ¾ inch) piece of foamcore
	Pushpin
	Scissors
	Wooden spool
	Colored pens, pencils, or crayons

Part 1: Assembling the Disk

1. Cut out the disk template below.
2. Place the template on the foamcore. Trace around the edge of the template.
3. Cut out the foamcore circle along the traced line. Trim off any rough edges.

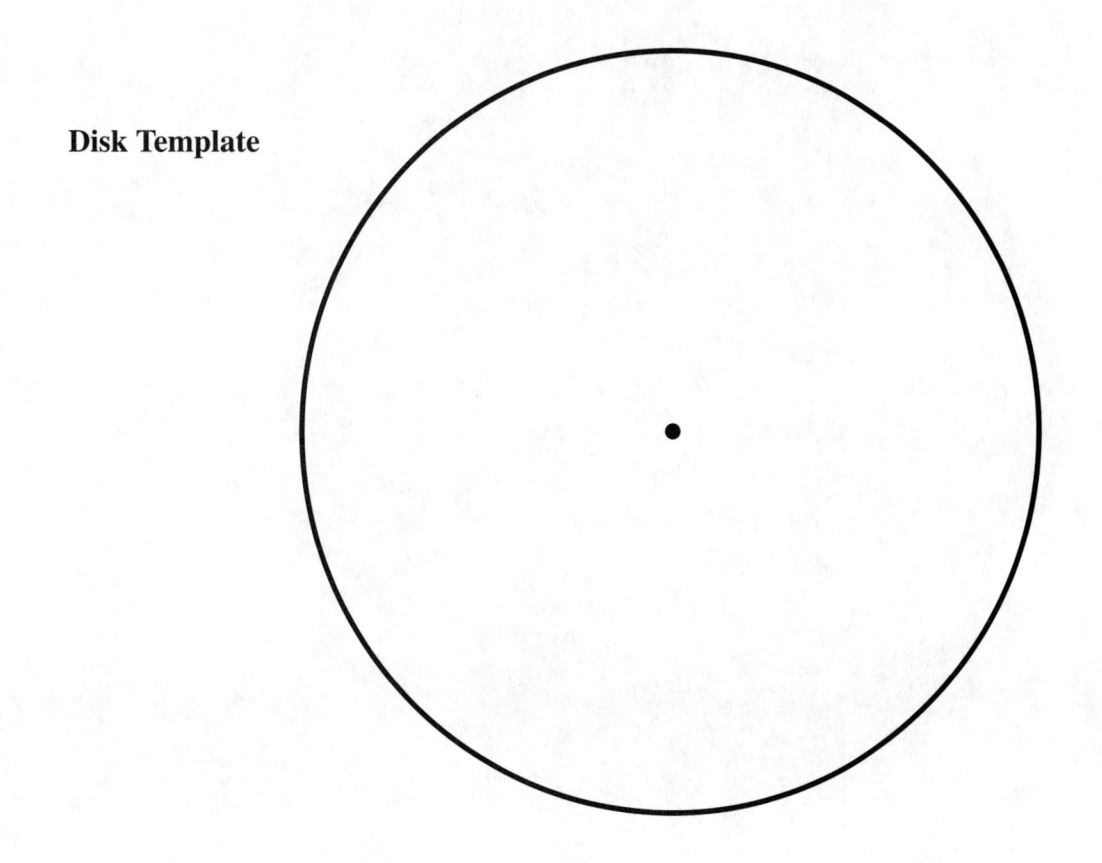

Disk Template

11

4. Lay the template back on the foamcore circle. Find the dot in the center of the template. Make a small hole with a pushpin through the dot, through the template, and all the way through the foamcore. When finished, take the pushpin and template off the foamcore.

5. Apply glue to one end of the spool without letting the glue go into the opening.

6. Place the spool on the foamcore (see Figure 1). Make sure the hole of the spool lines up with the hole made in the circle of foamcore.

7. Write your name on the top of the disk.

8. Using colored pens, pencils or crayons, decorate the top of your disk.

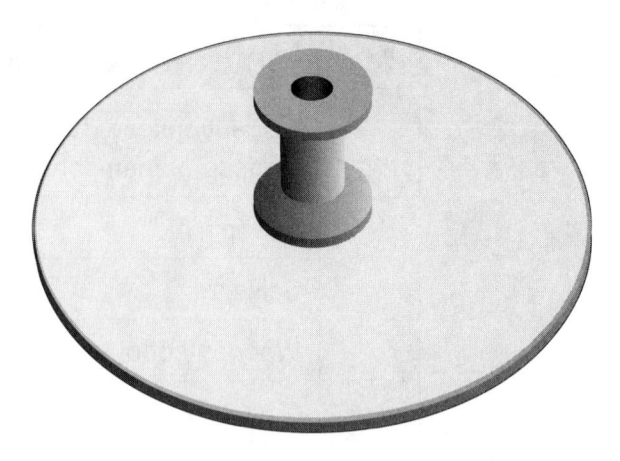

Figure 1: The spool glued to the foamcore.

Back of Disk Template

Part 2: Setting the Disk in Motion

Work with a partner to find three different strategies for making a disk move. Use the table below to record each strategy and to describe the disk's motion.

Strategies for Making a Disk Move

	Strategy for Moving Disk	Description of Disk's Motion
1		
2		
3		

INTERPRETING THE RESULTS

? 1. For each strategy you wrote in the table, what do you think limited how far the disk traveled?

_____

_____

? 2. What did you observe about the path of the disk in the trials?

_____

_____

? 3. Do you think you could get the disk to move in a curved path? If so, how?

_____

_____

? 4. For each strategy, how could you get the disk to move farther than it did?

_____

_____

? 5. What do you think caused the disk eventually to stop moving?

_____

_____

What I know about making an object move

_____

_____

_____

_____

14

Exploration 4: Launching the Super Sliding Disk

RECORDING YOUR IDEAS

1. If each time the disk were launched it moved the same distance, what could you infer about the push (force) that started the motion?

_____

_____

_____

_____

2. Can you think of a way to make sure that the disk goes the same distance each time it is launched?

_____

_____

_____

_____

3. My question about launching the disk is

_____

_____

_____

EXPLORATION 4 PROCEDURE

Collect the following materials with your partner.

✔	Materials Checklist
	Piece of corrugated cardboard, 17 centimeters x 13 centimeters (6 ¾ inches x 5 ⅛ inches)
	Scissors
	Large rubber band, 18 centimeters (about 7 inches) long
	Disks from Exploration 3
	Metric ruler

Part 1: Building the Disk Launcher

1. Cut out the launcher template on page 17.
2. Place the template on the cardboard so that the bottom outer edge is against one side of the cardboard. Trace around the template onto the cardboard to make a U-shaped launcher.
3. Cut out the cardboard launcher. Be careful not to bend the cardboard while cutting it. Save the scrap cardboard pieces for later.
4. Place your launcher and your partner's launcher together so they match up exactly.
5. Tape the launchers together with masking tape (see Figure 1).
6. Partner 1: Stretch about 4 centimeters (about 1 ½ inches) of the rubber band.

    Partner 2: Tape the stretched section of the rubber band to the bottom outer edge of the launcher (see Figure 2). Fit the rest of the rubber band around the outside of the launcher.

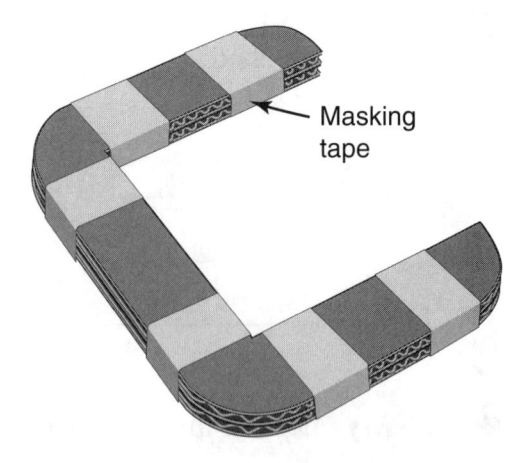

Figure 1: The cardboard launchers taped together.

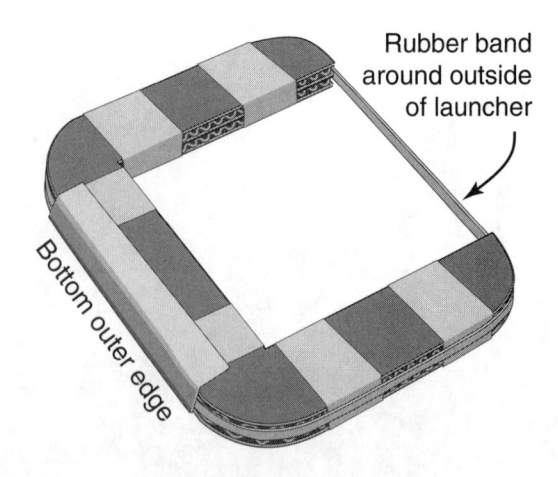

Figure 2: The rubber band taped to the bottom outer edge of the launcher.

7. Tape the rubber band in place (see Figure 3).

8. From the scraps of cardboard you saved, cut two cardboard rectangles, each measuring about 2.5 centimeters x 5 centimeters (1 inch x 2 inches).

9. Tape one rectangle about 2 centimeters (about ¾ inch) from the end of each leg of the launcher (see Figure 3). The rectangles are the feet of the launcher.

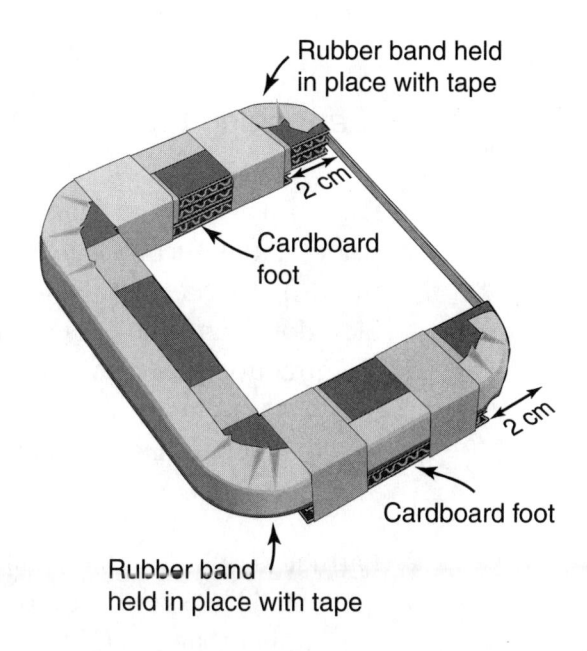

Figure 3: The disk launcher.

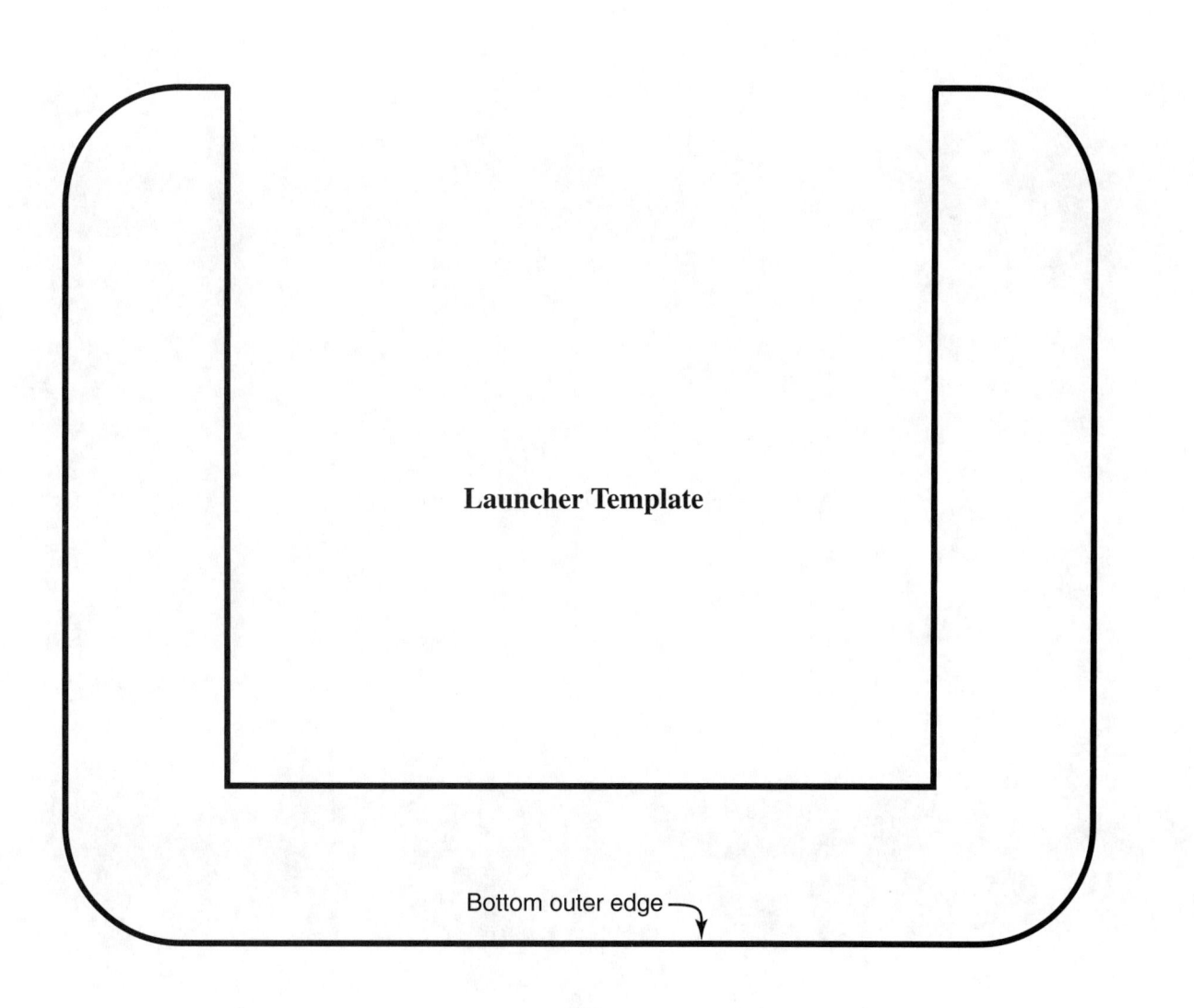

Launcher Template

Bottom outer edge

Part 2: Launching the Super Sliding Disk

1. Partner 1: Hold the launcher close to a smooth, flat surface, such as a table or floor. The feet of the launcher should face down and the legs should point in the direction you want the disk to move.

   ! Be considerate. Do not launch your disks at others.

2. Partner 2: Slide your disk under the launcher. The spool should pull back on the rubber band. Hold onto the foam base of the disk (not the spool) and pull the disk toward the base of the launcher (see Figure 4).

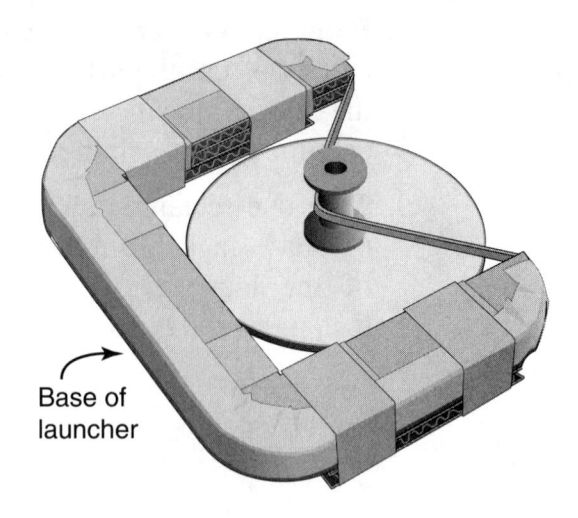

Figure 4: The disk pulled back in the launcher.

Back of Launcher Template

3. Partner 2: When you feel tension in the rubber band, release the disk.

4. Take turns launching your disks.

5. Investigate and describe how you can use your launcher to make the disk go farther.

   _____

   _____

   _____

6. Investigate and describe how you can use your launcher to make the disk go less far.

   _____

   _____

   _____

7. What strategies can you find to make your disk travel the same distance each time?

   _____

   _____

   _____

INTERPRETING THE RESULTS

? 1. How do you think the launcher can help you investigate motion?

_____
_____
_____

? 2. Does the amount of force used to start a disk in motion affect how far the disk moves? What is your evidence?

_____
_____
_____

? 3. How could you test your idea?

_____
_____
_____

? 4. Does the launcher give the disk a push or pull to start it moving?

_____
_____
_____

What I know about launching an object

_____
_____
_____
_____

Exploration 5: Testing the Limits of Your Launcher

RECORDING YOUR IDEAS

? 1. Where can you find a number scale?

_____
_____
_____

? 2. For what purposes can a number scale be used?

_____
_____
_____

? 3. Why might you want to add a number scale to your launcher?

_____
_____
_____

? 4. My question about adding a number scale to the launcher is

_____
_____
_____

FORCE FIELDS Launching a disk is similar to shooting an arrow from a bow. In the Olympics, archers shoot arrows at targets 70 meters (about 230 feet) away. From where the archers stand, the target looks as small as the head of a thumbtack held at arm's length. Modern arrows can travel more than 240 kilometers per hour (about 150 miles per hour).

EXPLORATION 5 PROCEDURE

Collect the following materials with your partner.

✔	Materials Checklist
	Disks
	Launcher
	Metric ruler
	Roll of adding machine paper
	Blue crayon / pen / pencil
	Red crayon / pen / pencil
	Green crayon / pen / pencil
	Tape measure
	Scissors

Part 1: Preparing the Number Scale

1. Place a ruler along the inner edge of one of the launcher's legs.
2. Mark and label every 2 centimeters along the leg from 2 centimeters to 6 centimeters (see Figure 1a). Do the same to the other leg.

   If you are using a non-metric ruler, mark and label 1 inch increments (see Figure 1b).

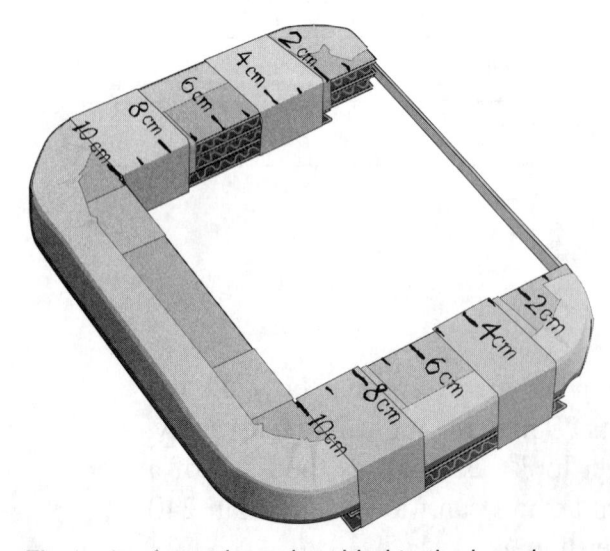

Figure 1a: A metric scale added to the launcher.

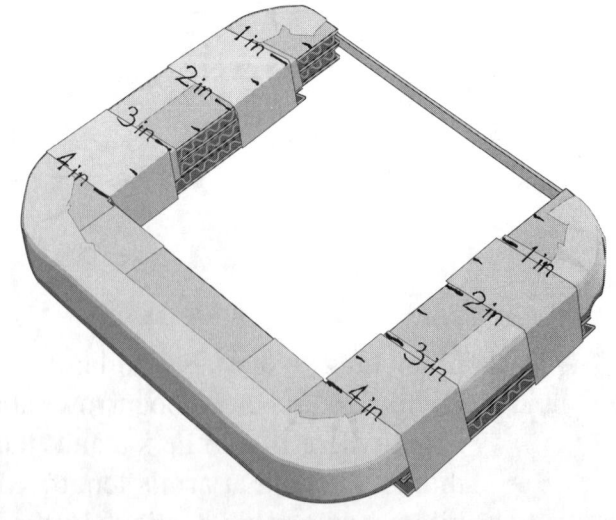

Figure 1b: A non-metric scale added to the launcher.

3. Find a smooth, level area on the floor or a cafeteria table that is approximately 3 meters (about 10 feet) long.

4. Measure and cut a 3 meter (about 10 foot) length of adding machine paper.

5. Tape the paper strip to the surface (see Figure 2).

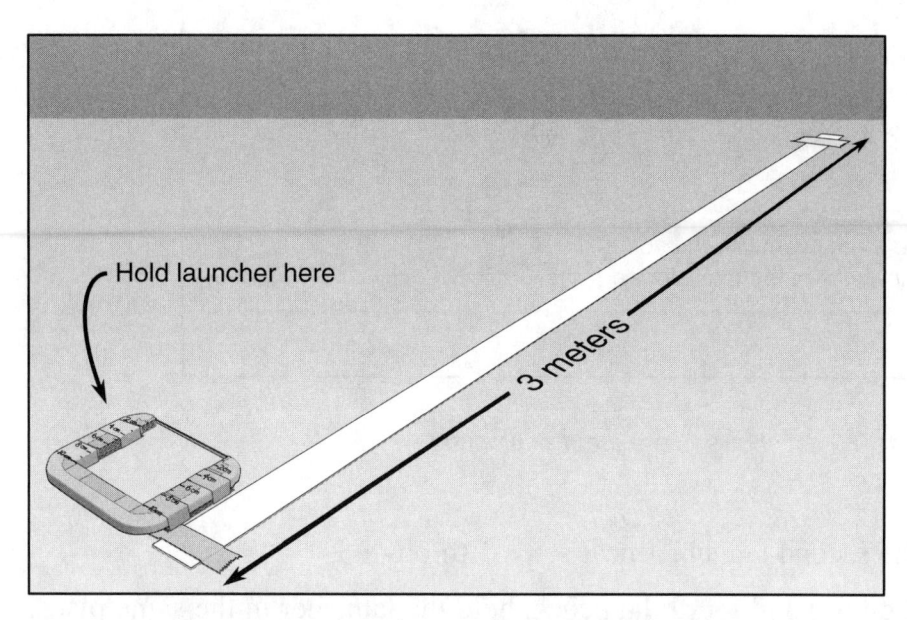

Figure 2: The paper strip taped to a flat, horizontal surface.

Part 2: Using the Scale

1. Partner 1: Hold the launcher close to the flat surface.

2. Partner 2: If you have a metric scale on your launcher, pull your disk back against the rubber band until the center of the spool is lined up with the 2 centimeter marks (see Figure 3). If you have a non-metric scale, pull the disk back to the 1 inch marks.

   Release the disk.

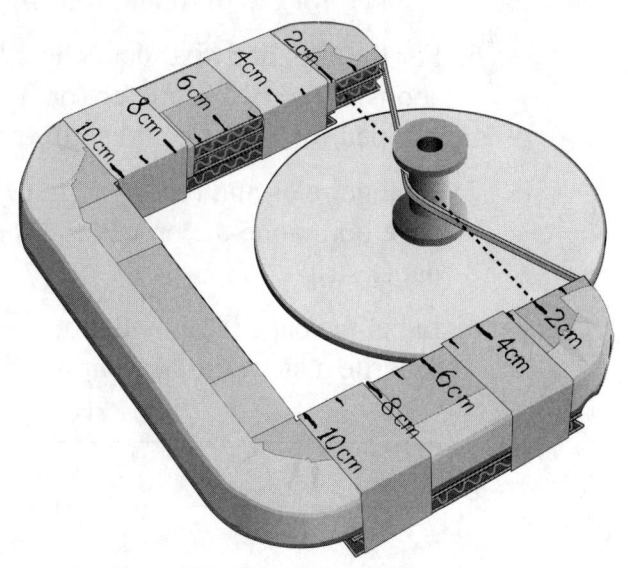

Figure 3: The disk pulled back to the 2 cm marks.

3. Both partners: After the disk has come to a complete stop, make a BLUE dot on the paper strip, lined up with the center of the disk's spool, to indicate where the disk stopped (see Figure 4).

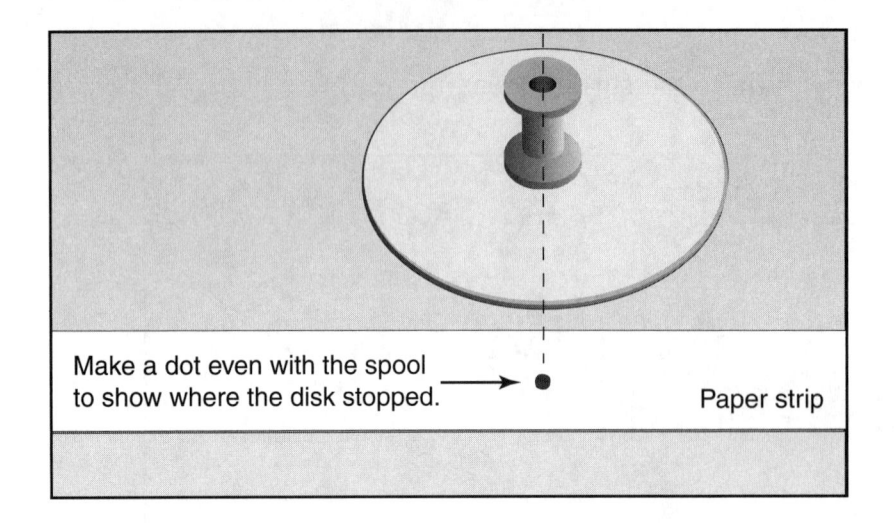

Figure 4: The dot shows where the disk stopped.

4. For the second launch, repeat steps 1 through 3.

5. For the third and fourth launches, hold the launcher in the same place, but pull the disk back against the rubber band until the spool is even with the 4 centimeter (or 2 inch) marks. Indicate where the disk stopped for the third and fourth trials with RED dots.

6. For the fifth and sixth launches, repeat the procedure, starting with the spool at the 6 centimeter (or 3 inch) marks. Indicate where the disk stopped for the fifth and sixth trials with GREEN dots.

7. Change roles and repeat steps 1 through 6. When your partner and you have both done the procedure, there should be a total of 12 dots on the paper strip.

8. Label the paper strip with your names and the date. Use the lines below to write a short description of what the dots represent.

INTERPRETING THE RESULTS

? 1. What do the different colored dots on your paper strip represent?

_____

_____

? 2. How does the motion of your disk change as you release it from farther back in the launcher?

_____

_____

? 3. Do you think there is a greater (stronger) or lesser (weaker) force applied to the disk the farther you pull it back in the launcher?

_____

? 4. Do you see any relationship between the calibrations (numbers) on the launcher and how far the disk goes? If so, what is it?

_____

_____

? 5. What evidence do you have for your answer?

_____

_____

What I know about how different forces affect motion

_____

_____

_____

_____

Exploration 6: There's a Lot of Friction in This World

RECORDING YOUR IDEAS

? 1. Do you think your disk would move farther if you launched it on a floor covered with a giant piece of sandpaper or a floor covered with ice? Why do you think so?

_____

_____

_____

? 2. What are some surfaces or materials that you could put on the floor to help make your disk move farther?

_____

_____

_____

? 3. What are some surfaces or materials that you could put on the floor to help make your disk move less far?

_____

_____

_____

? 4. My question about how surface texture affects motion is

_____

_____

_____

EXPLORATION 6 PROCEDURE

Part 1: Setting Up a Surface

Collect the following materials with your group.

✔	Materials Checklist
	Disks
	Roll of adding machine paper
	Disk launcher
	Tape measure
	Red crayon / pencil / pen
	Blue crayon / pencil / pen
	Scissors

1. Your teacher will tell you which test material to use. Measure and mark off or cut off a 6 meter (about 20 foot) length of the test material. Secure the material to the floor with masking tape.

2. Roll out and tape a 6 meter (about 20 foot) length of adding machine paper along one edge of the test material.

3. On one end of the paper strip, write what test material you are using.

Part 2: Testing a Surface

1. Student 1: Hold the launcher next to the labeled end of the paper strip.

2. Student 2: Pull your disk back against the rubber band to the 6 centimeter (or 3 inch) marks and launch the disk down the test surface.

3. Student 3: When the disk comes to a complete stop, mark an X on the paper strip with a pencil. Line up the X with the middle of the disk's spool to indicate the distance the disk moved.

4. Take turns until all group members have launched their disks down the test material. For each trial, make sure you hold the launcher at the same position.

5. You will now experiment with another group's test material. Leave your launcher and adding machine paper in place so that other groups can use them.

   Repeat steps 1 through 4 with the new test material, and then with the other materials.

6. When you have experimented with all of the test materials, return to your original test material.

   a) Which test material allowed the disks to travel the farthest?

   _____

   _____

   b) How can we use the paper strips to show which test material allowed the disks to travel the farthest?

   _____

   _____

   _____

7. Find the X that is the farthest from the launcher. Draw a RED line across the paper strip at this point.

   What does this line represent?

   _____

   How far is the red line from the end of the launcher?

   _____

8. Draw a BLUE line across the paper strip, so that half the X marks are on one side of the line and half are on the other.

   What does this line represent?

   _____

   How far is the blue line from the end of the launcher?

   _____

INTERPRETING THE RESULTS

Look at the markings on all of the paper strips, then answer the following questions:

1. On which surface did the disk travel the farthest? _____

2. On which surface did the disk travel least far? _____

3. Rank the materials in order of the distance the disk moved over them, from least far to farthest. How does this ranking compare to the predictions you made at the beginning of the exploration?

   _____
   _____
   _____

4. What can you infer about how different surfaces affect the distance the disk travels?

   _____
   _____
   _____

5. What can you infer about how different surfaces affect the strength of the friction acting on the disk?

   _____
   _____
   _____

What I know about how different surfaces can affect motion

_____
_____
_____
_____
_____

Exploration 7: Floating on Air

RECORDING YOUR IDEAS

? 1. What do you think the motion of the disk would be like if you could find a way to reduce the friction force acting on the disk?

___

? 2. What do you think stops a disk in motion from staying in motion forever?

___

? 3. What do you think keeps a hockey puck moving once it has been set in motion by a player?

___

? 4. My question about reducing the friction force is

___

FORCE FIELDS Curling, a sport that originated in Scotland, involves sliding a heavy, rounded, smooth stone on ice. Participants use brooms to sweep the ice in front of the sliding stones to increase their speed.

EXPLORATION 7 PROCEDURE

Part 1: Converting to an Air Disk

Collect the following materials with your partner.

✔	Materials Checklist
	Disks
	2 balloons

! For health reasons, do not share balloons.

1. Partner 1: Blow up a balloon until it is the size of a baseball or an orange. Twist the opening of the balloon closed so no air can escape. (Do not tie the balloon closed.)

2. Partner 2: Hold the foam base of your partner's disk on the table.

3. Partner 1: Attach the inflated balloon to the disk by carefully fitting the mouth of the balloon around the top of the spool (see Figure 1).

4. Partner 1: Make sure that the balloon is perpendicular to the disk (see Figure 1). When you let go of the balloon, air will flow out into the spool and through the the disk.

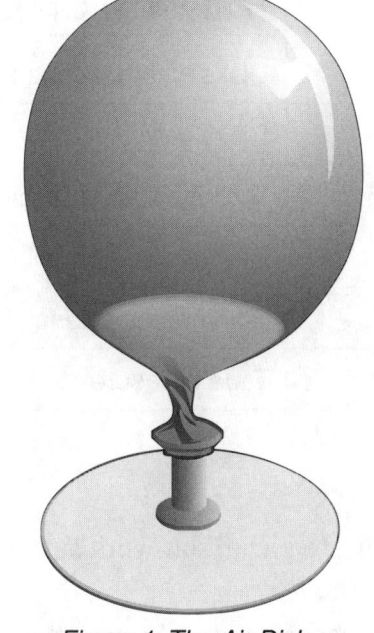

Figure 1: The Air Disk.

5. Both partners: Let go of the disk and the balloon at the same time.

6. Now convert Partner 2's disk into an Air Disk.

7. Investigate the motion of the Air Disks, then answer the following questions about your observations:

    a) Is the motion of the Air Disk the same as or different from the motion of a regular disk? If different, in what way is the motion different?

    _____
    _____
    _____

b) If you launched an Air Disk by pulling it back in a launcher 2 centimeters (or 1 inch), and a regular disk the same way, which would move farther?

_____

_____

Part 2: Testing the Air Disk

Collect the following materials with your partner.

✔	Materials Checklist
	Disks with balloons attached
	Disk launcher
	Roll of adding machine paper
	Red crayon / pencil / pen
	Blue crayon / pencil / pen
	Tape measure

1. Find a clean, flat work surface, about 6 meters (about 20 feet) in length.

2. Measure and cut a 6 meter (about 20 foot) length of adding machine paper.

3. Tape the paper strip to the edge of the work surface.

4. Partner 1: Hold the disk launcher at one end of the work surface.

5. Partner 2: Leave the uninflated balloon on your disk. Pull the disk back against the rubber band to the 2 centimeter (or 1 inch) marks and launch the disk.

6. Both partners: Mark a BLUE X on the paper strip where the disk stops. How far did the disk move?

   Trial 1: _____

7. Repeat steps 4 through 6 two more times for a total of three trials.

   Trial 2: _____

   Trial 3: _____

8. Switch roles and repeat the procedure with Partner 1's disk. How far did the disk move?

   Trial 1: _____

   Trial 2: _____

   Trial 3: _____

9. Partner 1: Hold the disk launcher in the same place.

10. Partner 2: Blow up your balloon until it is the size of a baseball. Twist the neck so no air escapes as you attach it to the spool of your disk.

11. Partner 2: Pull the Air Disk back against the rubber band to the 2 centimeter (or 1 inch) marks and launch the Air Disk.

12. Both partners: After the Air Disk comes to a complete stop, mark the distance it traveled by making a RED X on the paper strip.
    How far did the disk move?

    Trial 1: _____

13. Repeat steps 9 through 12 two more times.

    Trial 2: _____

    Trial 3: _____

14. Switch roles and repeat the procedure with Partner 1's Air Disk. How far did the disk move?

    Trial 1: _____

    Trial 2: _____

    Trial 3: _____

INTERPRETING THE RESULTS

1. In what ways did the air cushion change the disk's motion?

2. To go any specific distance, does the Air Disk need to be launched with as strong a force as the original disk? What is the basis for your answer?

3. Why do you think the Air Disk eventually stopped moving?

4. Once an object is in motion it seems to stay in motion, neither speeding up nor slowing down, unless a force (push or pull) acts on it. Scientists call this behavior *inertia*. Does your Air Disk exhibit inertia? If so, how?

What I know about friction

Unit 3: ROLLING MOTION ON AN INCLINED PLANE

Exploration 8: Setting Up the Track

RECORDING YOUR IDEAS

1. Imagine a child is sitting at the top of a slide. Then the child starts to go down the slide. Why do you think the child keeps moving?

_____
_____
_____

2. Do you think the speed of the child increases or stays the same during a ride down the slide? Why do you think so?

_____
_____
_____

3. If the child goes down the slide and lands on his or her feet at the bottom, is there any further motion? Why or why not?

_____
_____
_____

4. My question about motion on a slide is

_____
_____
_____

EXPLORATION 8 PROCEDURE

Collect the following materials with your group.

✔	Materials Checklist
	6 regular tracks
	Red-ended track
	6 regular connectors
	Black-ended connector
	Paper cup
	Piece of card stock or file folder, 21.5 centimeters x 28 centimeters (8½ inches x 11 inches), for each member of your group
	Metric ruler
	Scissors
	12 plastic marbles of the same size

Part 1: Building a Track Tower

Each member of the group will make a Track Tower. When you are finished with this unit, you can take home the tower and use it to share what you know with your family and friends.

1. Cut out the Track Tower template on page 37.

2. Glue the Track Tower template, face up, onto the card stock or file folder.

3. Cut out the template from the card stock or file folder.

4. Fold the template inward along the dotted lines. Crease the folds.

5. Arrange the template so that you have a box shape with four long sides and two open ends. Tape the flap over the side (see Figure 1).

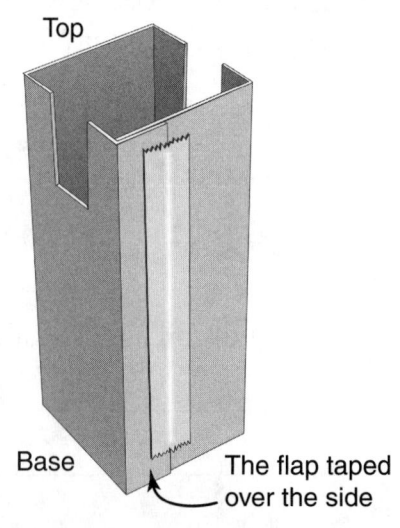

Figure 1: The Track Tower.

Flap

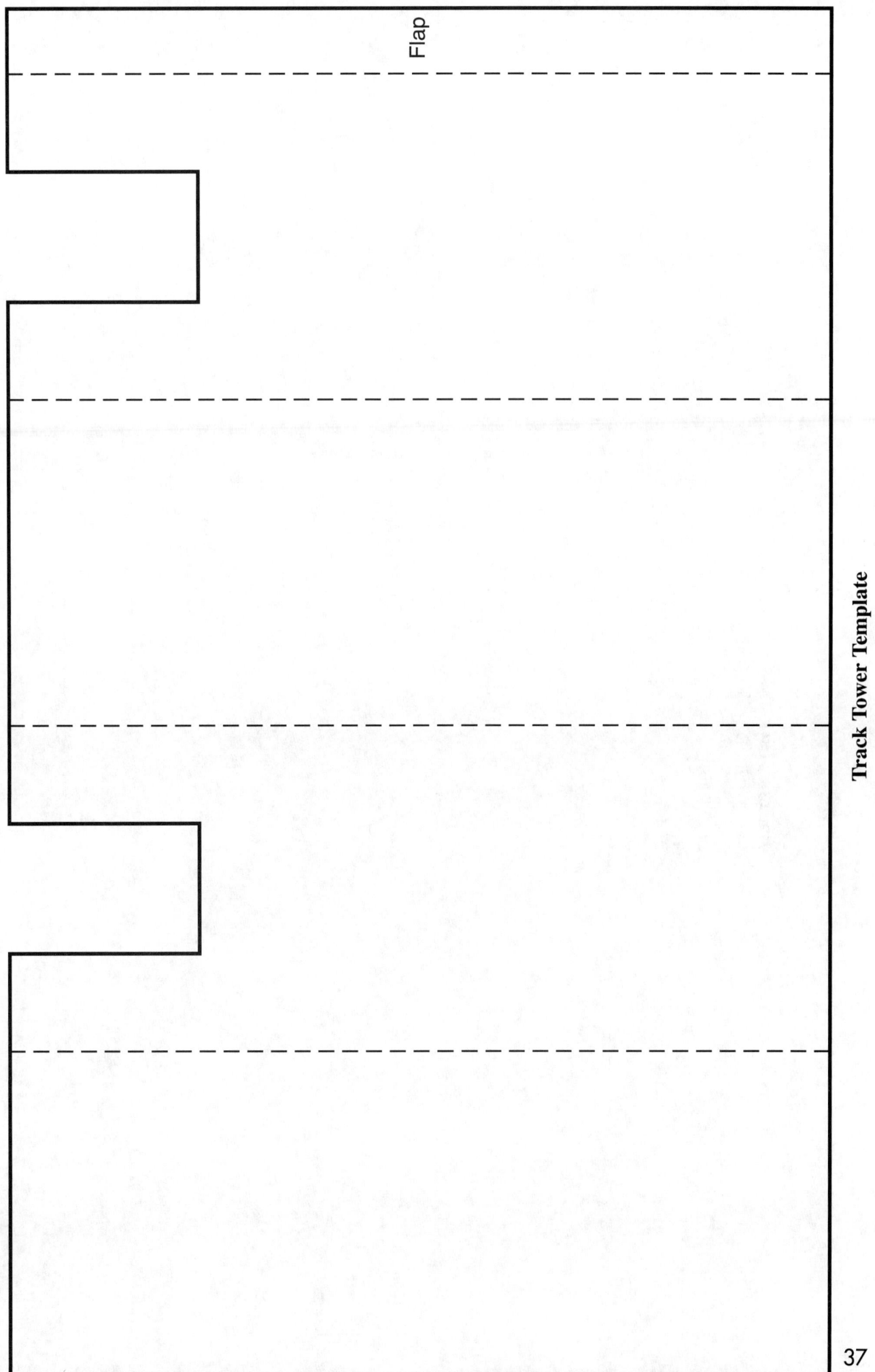

Track Tower Template

37

Back of Track Tower Template

Part 2: Preparing the Flat Track

You will now set up the flat track with your group.

1. Place the black-ended connector, base-down, on a flat surface. Push one regular track into the connector. The base and walls of the connector should wrap around the base and walls of the track (see Figure 2).

2. Slide the connector along the track until only the black portion extends beyond the end of the track (see Figure 2).

3. Take a regular connector and nest the opposite end of the track into the connector.

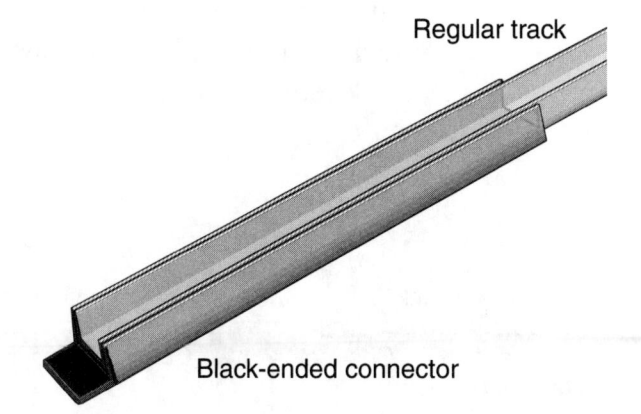

Figure 2: The black-ended connector attached to one regular track.

4. Slide the connector along the base of the track so that about half of the connector extends from the end of the track.

5. Take a second track and nest it into the connector. Push the two pieces of track together so that their ends are flush against each other at about the middle of the connector (see Figure 3).

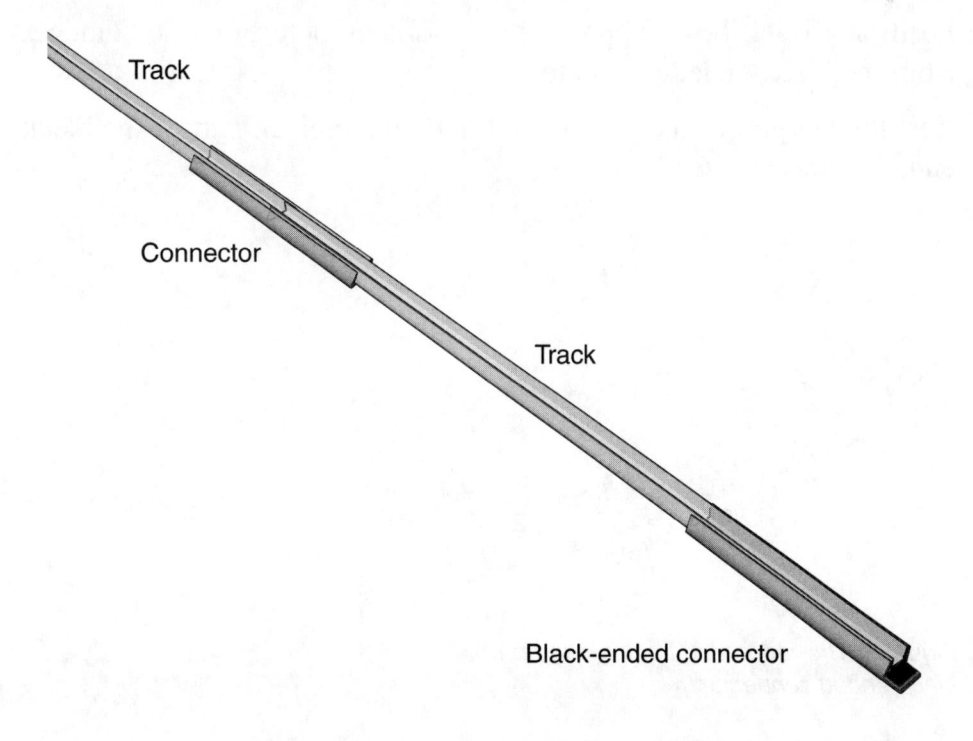

Figure 3: Two tracks joined with a connector.

6. Connect four more regular tracks using the same method, so that you have a total of six tracks connected (see Figure 4).

7. Attach one more connector to the free end of the sixth track. No other tracks will be added. This last connector is simply attached to help the track remain stable. The flat track is now complete (see Figure 4).

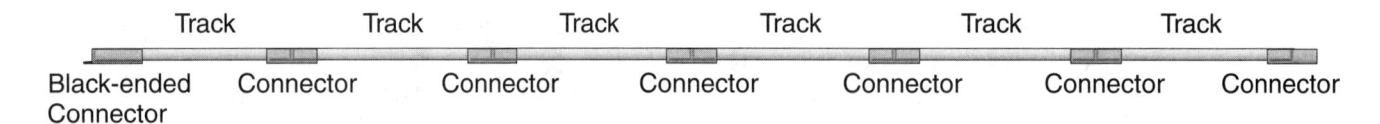

Figure 4: The flat track.

Part 3: Putting It All Together

1. Lay the flat track, base-down, on a floor or other flat work area at least 4 meters (about 13 feet) long.

2. Position a Track Tower approximately 57 centimeters (about 22 inches) from the black-ended connector.

3. Rest the red part of the red-ended track on the black part of the black-ended connector (see Figure 5).

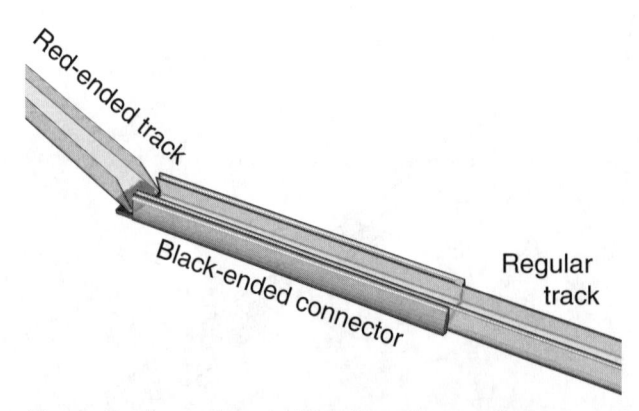

Figure 5: The red-ended track resting on the black-ended connector.

4. Rest the opposite end of the red-ended track in one of the rectangle cutouts of the Track Tower (see Figure 6).

5. You now have an inclined track leading to a flat track (see Figure 7). Check to see that all six track pieces of the flat track are flush against each other.

6. At the very end of the flat track, tape a paper cup to the work surface to catch marbles that roll down the track (see Figure 7).

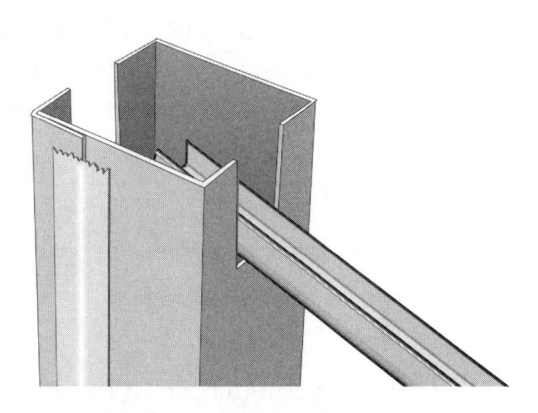

Figure 6: The opposite end of the red-ended track resting in the Track Tower.

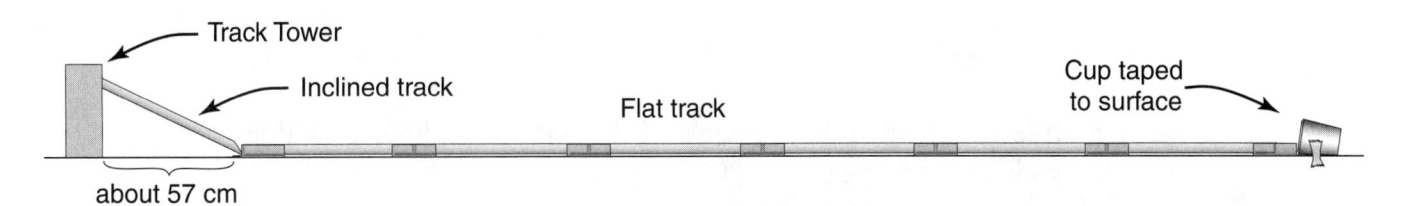

Track Tower
Inclined track
Flat track
Cup taped to surface
about 57 cm

Figure 7: The track setup.

Part 4: The Marbles Roll

1. Predict what would happen if you set a marble on the track.

   a) What do you predict would happen if you placed a marble halfway up the inclined track and then let go of it?

   b) How far would the marble roll? Describe how you made this prediction.

c) Do you think the marble would move differently if you started it near the bottom of the inclined track instead of near the top of the inclined track? Why do you think so?

_____

_____

_____

2. Set a marble in the middle of the incline and allow it to roll down and along the flat track. Repeat this several times.

3. What did you observe about the motion of the marble?

_____

_____

4. Set a marble at the top of the incline and allow it to roll down and along the flat track several times.

5. What did you observe about the motion of the marble?

_____

_____

6. Set a marble near the bottom of the incline and allow it to roll down and along the flat track several times.

7. What did you observe about the motion of the marble?

_____

_____

8. Discuss the following question with the other members of your group:

- When you started a marble at the same point on the incline, did it roll the exact same distance each time? Why do you think the marble behaved as it did?

INTERPRETING THE RESULTS

1. Did you notice a difference in the motion of a marble when it started near the top of the incline instead of near the bottom of the incline? Describe what you observed.

_____

_____

_____

2. Write a sentence that compares the motion of a marble when it starts near the bottom of the incline to the motion when it starts near the top of the incline.

_____

_____

_____

3. What is different about a marble rolling down an incline from a marble rolling along a horizontal track? What do you think accounts for this difference?

_____

_____

_____

What I know about the motion of an object rolling down an incline

Exploration 9: How Far Does It Roll?

RECORDING YOUR IDEAS

? 1. Prediction: The higher up along the inclined track a marble starts, the farther it will roll along the horizontal, flat track.

How could you test this prediction?

_____
_____
_____
_____

? 2. What measuring tool(s) would you use?

_____
_____
_____
_____

? 3. My question about how starting height affects the distance an object moves is

_____
_____
_____
_____

EXPLORATION 9 PROCEDURE

Collect the following materials with your group.

✔	Materials Checklist
	Track setup (6 regular tracks, 6 regular connectors, black-ended connector, red-ended track, Track Tower, paper cup)
	12 plastic marbles of the same size
	2 tape measures
	Metric ruler or another tape measure

Part 1: Attaching the Tape Measure to the Inclined Track

1. Turn the red-ended track upside down, so that it rests on its walls. Lay a tape measure *metric side down* along the base of the red-ended track (see Figure 1a). Orient the tape measure so that its beginning (the number zero) is aligned with the red mark at the end of the track.

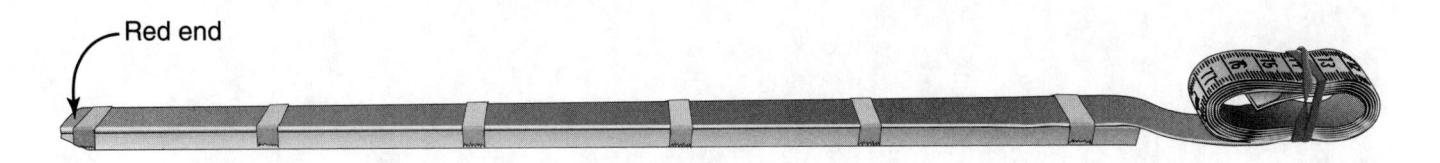

Figure 1a: The tape measure attached to the red-ended track, with zero at the red end.

2. Secure the tape measure in position with masking tape. Make sure the tape does not overlap the inside walls of the track. When you turn the track over, you should be able to see the metric calibrations of the tape measure through the clear plastic base of the track (see Figure 1b).

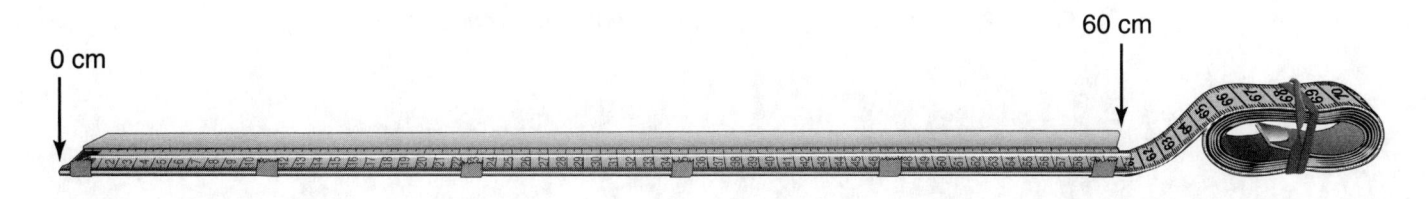

Figure 1b: The metric calibrations (in centimeters) showing through the base of the track.

3. The tape measure will most likely be longer than the track. Roll up the extra tape measure and secure it with masking tape or a rubber band (see Figures 1a and 1b).

4. Set up the track as you did in the last exploration. You can put the rolled-up part of the tape measure in the center of the Track Tower (see Figure 2).

Part 2: Attaching the Tape Measure to the Work Surface

1. Lay a second tape measure on the work surface, *metric side up*.

2. Position the tape measure along the side of the flat track, about 2 centimeters (about ¾ inch) from the track. Line up its beginning (the number zero) with the point where the inclined track meets the flat track (see Figure 2).

3. Use masking tape to secure the tape measure to the work surface.

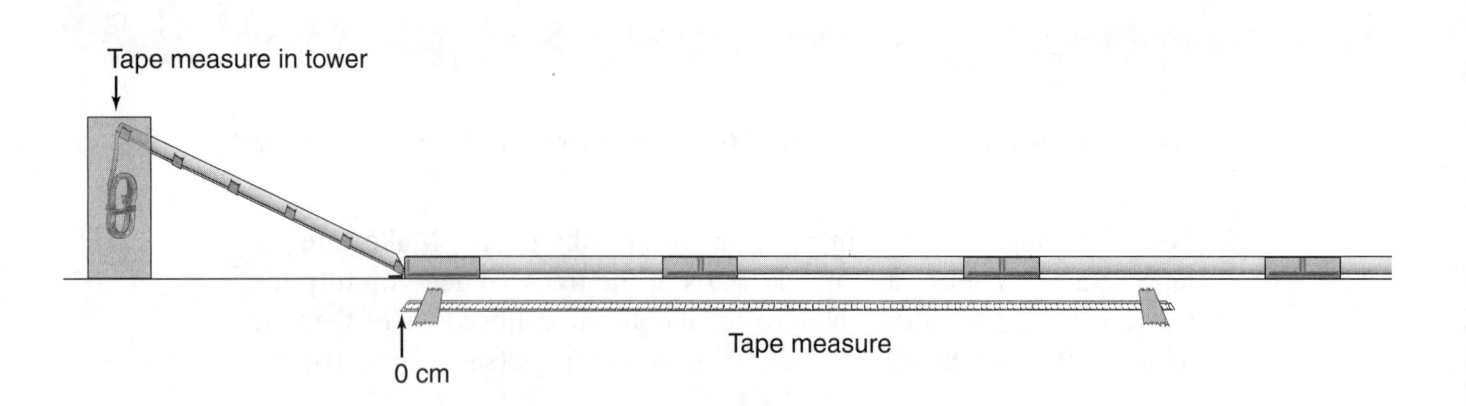

Figure 2: The second tape measure taped to the work surface.

Part 3: Starting the Marbles

1. Choose two Starters, two Measurers, two Recorders, and two Track Inspectors.

2. Track Inspectors: Before each trial, inspect the track to see that it is straight and that all the track pieces are flush. Remove any lint you see on the track.

3. Starters: Place a marble 10 centimeters up the inclined track (see Figure 3).

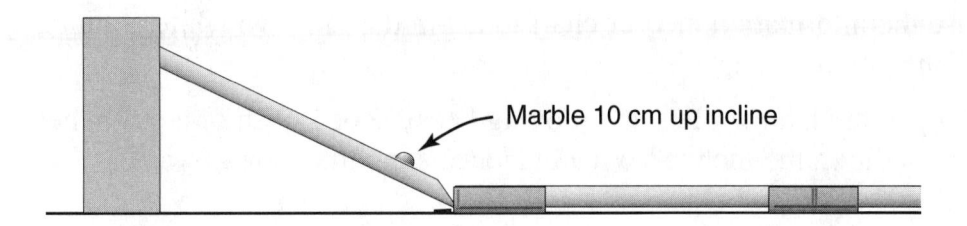

Figure 3: A marble placed 10 centimeters up the inclined track.

4. Starters: When all group members are ready, one Starter releases the marble and allows it to roll down the incline and along the flat track.

   In order to release the marble without accidentally giving it a push, hold a pencil in front of the marble and lift it to allow the marble to roll.

5. Measurers: After the marble has stopped, measure the distance the marble rolled along the flat track. If the marble rolled beyond the end of the tape measure, use a metric ruler or another tape measure to continue measuring.

6. Recorders: Record the measurement in the first column of the chart below.

Distance a Marble Rolls Starting from 10 and 20 cm up the Track

| | Distance Marble Rolls (in cm) ||
	Starting 10 cm up	Starting 20 cm up
Trial 1		
Trial 2		
Trial 3		
Average		

7. Repeat steps 2 through 6 two more times until your group has made three measurements and recorded them in the chart.

8. Share the data from the Recorders' charts. Find the average of the three measurements and compare your answers. Enter the average on your chart.

9. For the next three trials, you will use the same procedure. It is a good idea to switch jobs so different group members can have a chance to be the Starters, Measurers, Recorders, and Track Inspectors. The Starters will start a marble 20 centimeters up the inclined track. Record the results in the appropriate column of the chart.

10. Use the information in your chart to fill in the first two white columns of the graph on page 49.

11. Do you think a marble starts moving because of a push or a pull when you set it on the incline? What evidence supports your answer?

   _____

   _____

   _____

12. What do we commonly call the force that starts a marble moving down an incline?

   _____

   _____

48

Bar Graph of the Relationship Between Starting Height and Distance

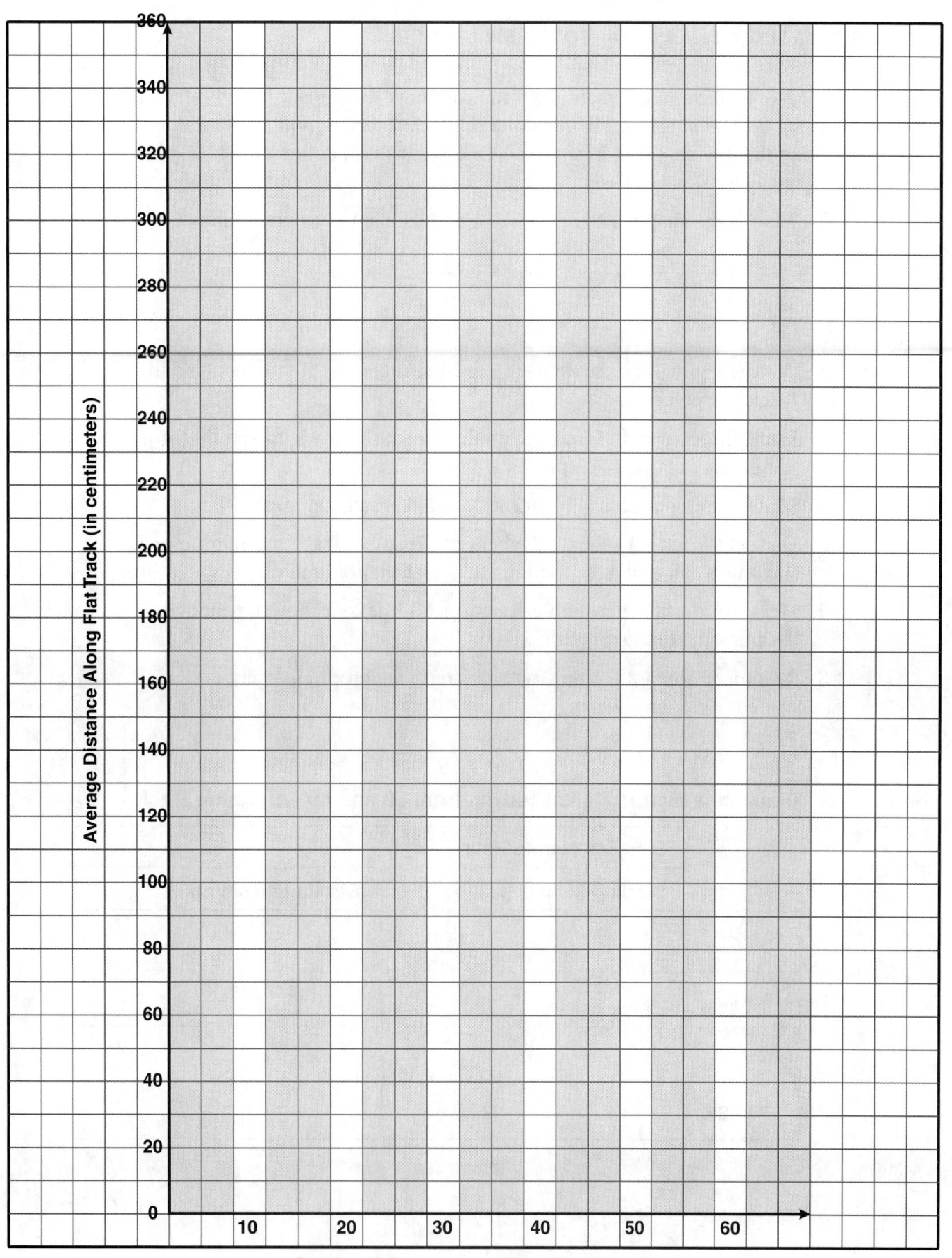

Y-axis: Average Distance Along Flat Track (in centimeters) — 0 to 360

X-axis: Starting Height up the Incline (in centimeters) — 0 to 60

Part 4: The Marbles Roll from New Heights

1. Use your graph to predict how far you think a marble will roll when it starts 30 centimeters, 40 centimeters, 50 centimeters, and 60 centimeters up the incline. Draw a horizontal line across each column to show your predictions.

2. What is the shape of the graph that results from your predictions?

_____

_____

3. Decide who will be the Starters, the Measurers, the Recorders, and the Track Inspectors.

4. Track Inspectors: Before each trial, inspect the track to see that it is straight and all the track pieces are flush.

5. Starters: Set a marble 30 centimeters up the inclined track.

6. Starters: When all group members are ready, release the marble and allow it to roll down the incline and along the flat track.

7. Measurers: After the marble has stopped, measure how far along the flat track the marble rolled.

8. Recorders: Record the measurement in the appropriate chart.

Distance a Marble Rolls Starting from 30 and 40 cm up the Track

	Distance Marble Rolls (in cm)	
	Starting 30 cm up	Starting 40 cm up
Trial 1		
Trial 2		
Trial 3		
Average		

Distance a Marble Rolls Starting from 50 and 60 cm up the Track

	Distance Marble Rolls (in cm)	
	Starting 50 cm up	Starting 60 cm up
Trial 1		
Trial 2		
Trial 3		
Average		

9. Repeat steps 4 through 8 two more times until your group has made and recorded three measurements.

10. Share the data from the Recorders' charts. Find the average of the three measurements and compare your answers. Enter the average in your chart.

11. Use the information in your chart to fill in the appropriate column of the graph on page 49.

12. Repeat the procedure three more times. The Starters will start a marble 40 centimeters, 50 centimeters, and then 60 centimeters up the inclined track.

13. If your group finishes early, try the following challenge:

    Can you use the information recorded on your graph to find a way to make a marble roll exactly 100 centimeters along the flat track? (Do not use a barricade to stop the marble.)

    Test your ideas and record successful methods below.

    _____
    _____
    _____
    _____
    _____

INTERPRETING THE RESULTS

? 1. What does your graph show you?

_____

_____

? 2. Why do you think the columns are of different heights?

_____

_____

? 3. How could you use the graph to predict how far a marble would roll if it started 45 centimeters up the incline?

_____

_____

? 4. Does the overall shape of your graph tell you anything you didn't know before? If so, what?

_____

_____

_____

What I know about how starting height affects rolling distance

_____

_____

_____

_____

_____

Exploration 10: How Fast Does It Roll?

RECORDING YOUR IDEAS

? 1. Prediction: The higher up along the inclined track a marble starts, the faster it will roll along the horizontal, flat track.

How could you test this prediction?

_____

_____

_____

? 2. What measuring tool(s) would you use?

_____

_____

_____

? 3. My question about timing the motion of a moving object is

_____

_____

_____

FORCE FIELDS At the annual Soapbox Derby in Akron, Ohio, participants in their carts coast 300 meters (about 1,000 feet) down the side of a hill from a standing start. By the time the carts cross the finish line at the bottom of the hill, they are traveling nearly 50 kilometers per hour (about 30 miles per hour).

EXPLORATION 10 PROCEDURE

Part 1: Practicing Timing

Collect the following materials with your group. Each group will need one member who has a watch that can be used to time the trials to at least tenths of a second.

✔	Materials Checklist
	Track setup (3 regular tracks, 3 regular connectors, black-ended connector, red-ended track, Track Tower, paper cup)
	Tape measure
	6 plastic marbles of the same size

1. Set up a flat track consisting of three regular tracks, three regular connectors, and a black-ended connector (see Figure 1).

2. If the red-ended track does not have an attached tape measure, tape one on as in the last exploration. Choose one Track Tower and use it to support the inclined red-ended track (see Figure 1).

3. Tape a cup at the end of the flat track and a tape measure alongside the flat track (see Figure 1).

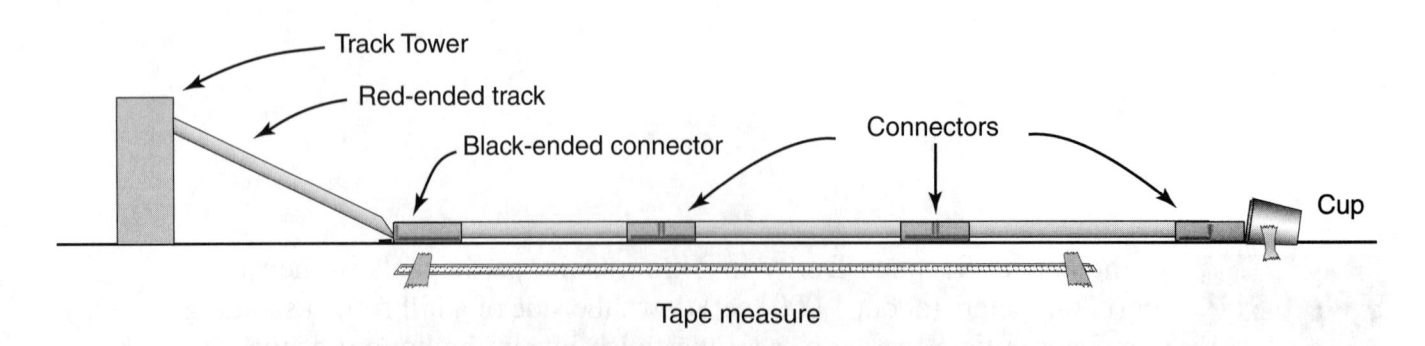

Figure 1: Setup showing how to connect three pieces of track.

4. Start a marble 30 centimeters up the incline and use a watch or stopwatch to measure how long it takes for the marble to roll 100 centimeters along the flat track. Start timing when the marble reaches the bottom of the incline. Stop timing when the marble reaches the 100 centimeter mark.

How long did the marble take? _____

Part 2: Assembling Bell Stands

Collect the following materials with your group.

✔	Materials Checklist
	8 large paper clips
	Drinking straw
	4 small rubber bands
	4 small metal bells
	Scissors
	Metric ruler

Each of the four members of your group needs to make one bell stand.

1. Slip one end of the rubber band though the hook on the top of the bell. The rubber band should now have two loops, one on either side of the bell hook (see Figure 2a). Pull one loop through the other loop until the rubber band is securely fastened to the bell hook (see Figure 2b).

2. Bend the two large paper clips open until each forms a 90 degree angle.

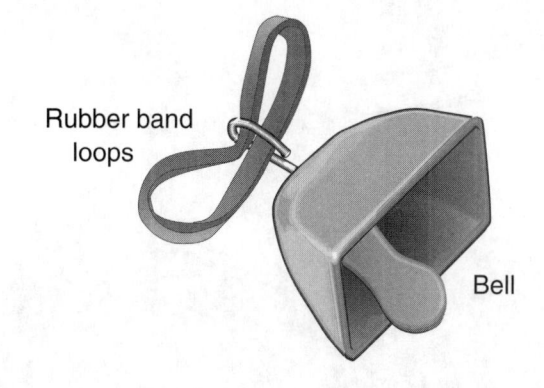

Figure 2a: The two loops of the rubber band.

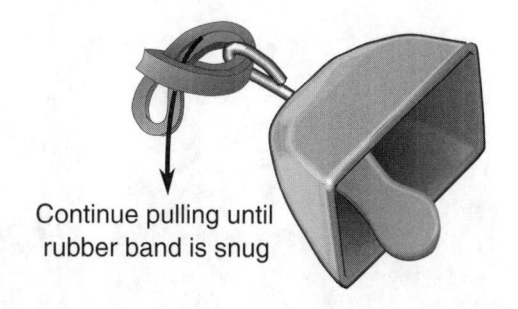

Figure 2b: One loop pulled through the other.

3. A bent paper clip has two hooks, one wider and one narrower. Hold the rubber band attached to the bell under the wide hook so that the rubber band is on one side of the hook and the bell is on the other side (see Figure 3a).

   Lift the bell up and over the hook, and through the rubber band loop. Pull the bell until the rubber band is snug (see Figure 3b).

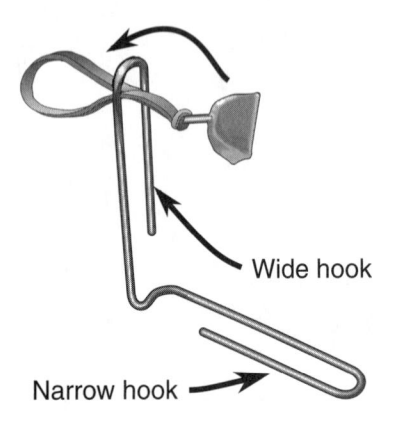

Figure 3a: Paper clip hook with rubber band and bell.

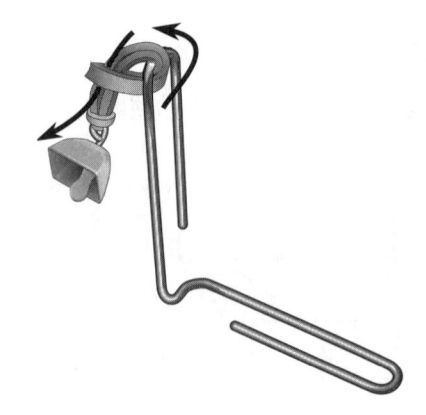

Figure 3b: How to attach the bell to the paper clip.

4. Measure and cut the drinking straw into 4 centimeter (about 1½ inch) pieces. Four students can share one straw.

5. Push the narrow hook of the paper clip with the bell into one end of the drinking straw.

6. Push the narrow hook of the second bent paper clip into the opposite end of the drinking straw.

7. Turn the straw and paper clips so the two wide hooks point in opposite directions, as shown in Figure 4.

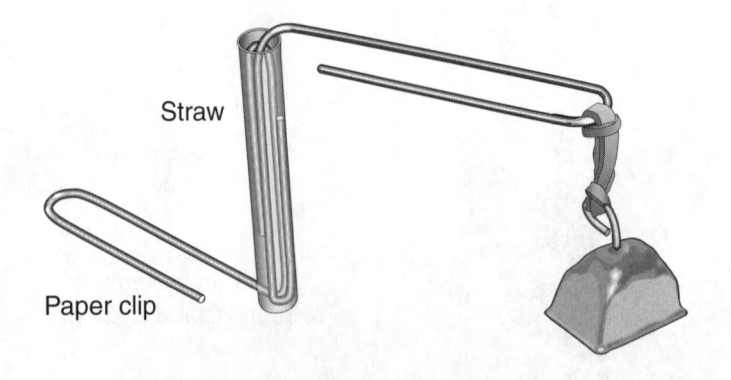

Figure 4: A completed bell stand.

Part 3: Setting Up the Bell Stands

1. Hold each bell stand so that the bell hangs over the track and the bottom part of the stand rests flat on the work surface (see Figure 5).

2. Tape the bell stand in this position with masking tape (see Figure 5).

3. Adjust the bell so it rings when a marble rolls along the track under the bell. The marble should hit only the clapper of the bell. Raise or lower the top paper clip in the straw to raise or lower the bell, or move the rubber band to adjust where the bell hangs.

4. Set up all four bell stands along the track.

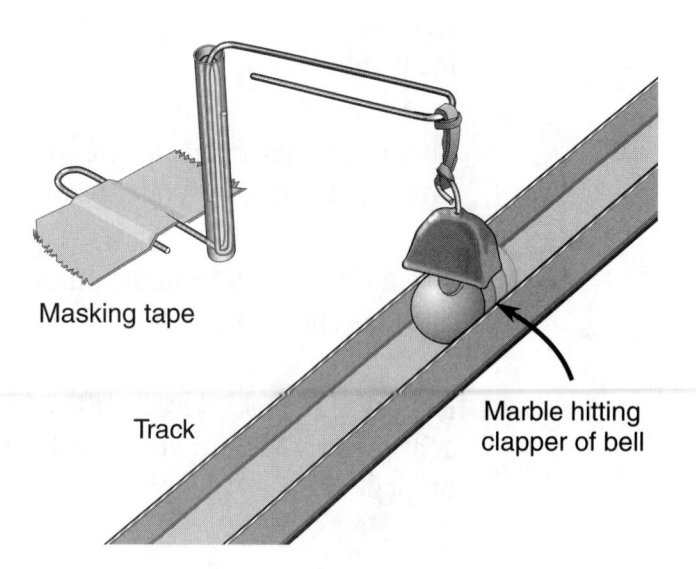

Figure 5: A bell stand taped in position alongside the track.

Part 4: Timing a Marble

1. Set up your track with two bell stands, one at 0 centimeters and one at 100 centimeters along the flat track.

2. Decide who will be the Starter, the Timer, the Recorder, and the Track Inspector.

3. Track Inspector: Before each trial, inspect the track to see that it is straight, the track pieces are flush, and the bells are hanging properly.

4. Starter: Set a marble 60 centimeters up the inclined track. When all group members are ready, release the marble and allow it to roll down the incline to the flat track.

5. Timer: As the marble rings the first bell, start the stopwatch. As the marble rings the second bell, stop the stopwatch.

6. Recorder: Record the time in the chart below.

7. Repeat steps 3 through 6 until you have made and recorded three measurements.

8. Share the data from the Recorder's chart. Average together the three times, and compare your answers. Enter the average in the chart below.

9. Use the information in the chart below to fill in the appropriate column of the graph on page 60.

10. Repeat the procedure until you have completed three trials at 50 centimeters. Record your results in the chart below and graph your data on page 60.

Time a Marble Takes to Roll 100 cm Starting from 60 and 50 cm

	Time Marble Takes to Roll 100 cm (in seconds)	
	Starting 60 cm up the incline	**Starting 50 cm up the incline**
Trial 1		
Trial 2		
Trial 3		
Average		

11. Repeat the procedure until you have completed three trials at 40 centimeters and three trials at 30 centimeters. Record your results in the chart below and graph your data on page 60.

Time a Marble Takes to Roll 100 cm Starting from 40 and 30 cm

| | Time Marble Takes to Roll 100 cm (in seconds) ||
	Starting 40 cm up the incline	Starting 30 cm up the incline
Trial 1		
Trial 2		
Trial 3		
Average		

12. Repeat the procedure, starting a marble at 20 centimeters, then at 10 centimeters. Record your results in the chart below and add your data to the graph on page 60.

Time a Marble Takes to Roll 100 cm Starting from 20 and 10 cm

| | Time Marble Takes to Roll 100 cm (in seconds) ||
	Starting 20 cm up the incline	Starting 10 cm up the incline
Trial 1		
Trial 2		
Trial 3		
Average		

Bar Graph of the Relationship Between Starting Height and Time

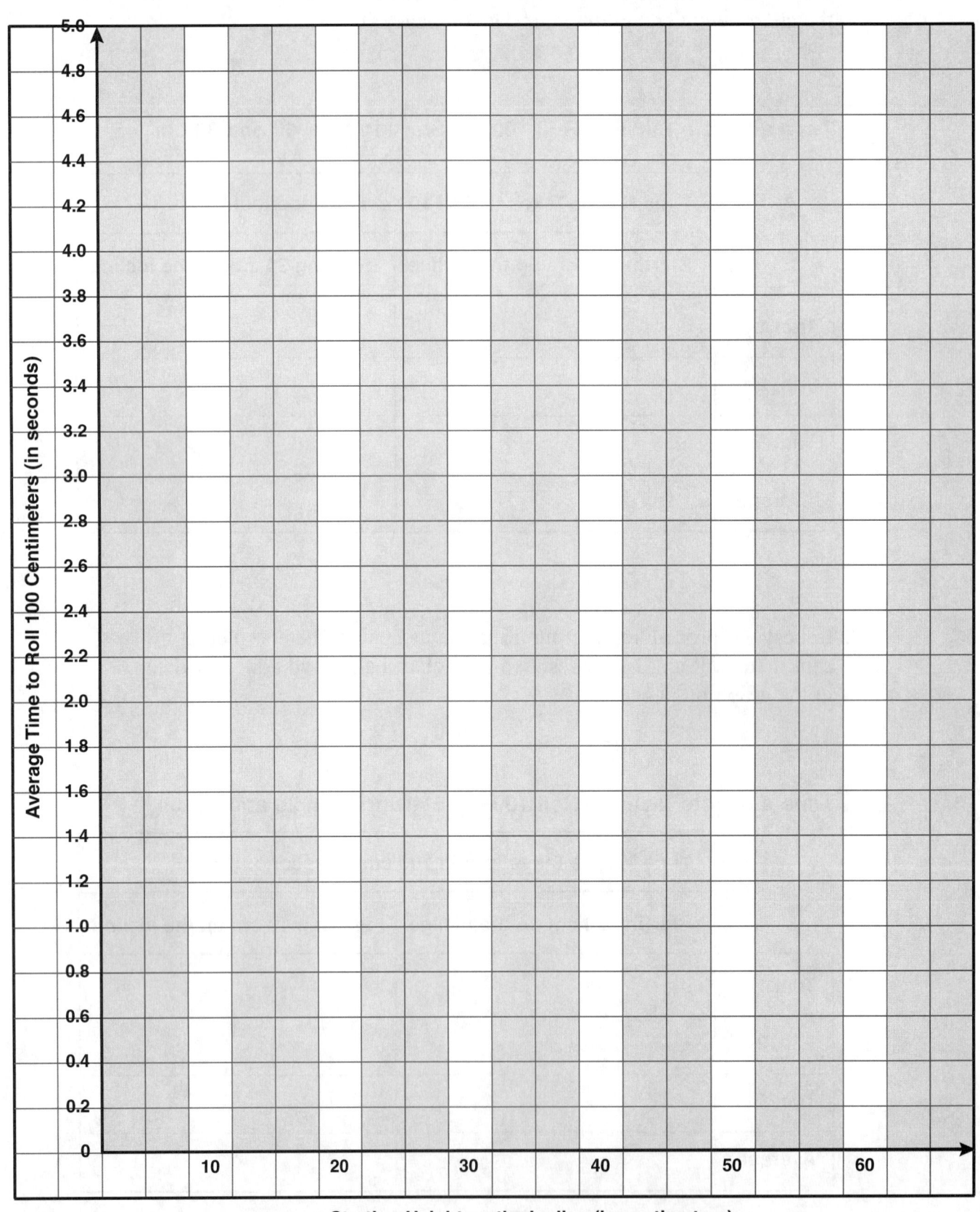

y-axis: Average Time to Roll 100 Centimeters (in seconds), 0 to 5.0

x-axis: Starting Height up the Incline (in centimeters), 0 to 60

INTERPRETING THE RESULTS

1. What does the shape of your graph tell you about the behavior of a ball that rolls down an inclined track onto a horizontal track?

_____
_____
_____

2. How could you use the graph to predict what would happen if you started a marble at a new point on the incline?

_____
_____
_____
_____

3. How can the graph help you predict the behavior of a different ball that rolls down an inclined track?

_____
_____
_____
_____

What I know about how starting height affects rolling speed

_____
_____
_____
_____

Exploration 11: Rolling Speed Along a Horizontal Track

RECORDING YOUR IDEAS

? 1. Think of your track setup. After a marble rolls down the incline, do you think it speeds up, slows down, or moves at a constant speed as it rolls along the flat track? (See Figure 1.)

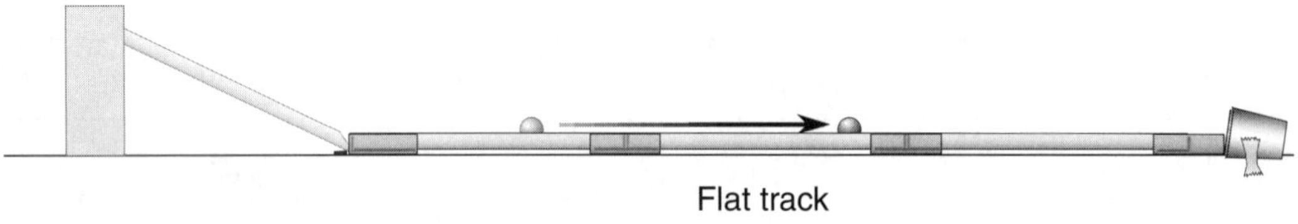

Figure 1: The marble rolling along the flat track.

? 2. Why do you think so?

? 3. What evidence could you obtain to test your answer?

? 4. My question about determining if an object is speeding up, slowing down, or moving at a constant speed is

EXPLORATION 11 PROCEDURE

Collect the following materials with your group. Each group will need one member who has a watch that can be used to time the trials to at least tenths of a second.

✔	Materials Checklist
	Track setup (3 regular tracks, 3 regular connectors, black-ended connector, red-ended track with tape measure attached, Track Tower, paper cup)
	6 plastic marbles of the same size
	4 bell stands
	Tape measure

1. Set up the track with a tape measure taped parallel to the flat track.
2. Set up bell stands at 0 centimeters and 100 centimeters along the flat track.
3. Make three equal segments of track by setting up the remaining two bell stands at 50 centimeters and 150 centimeters (see Figure 2).
4. Decide who will be the Starter, the Timer, the Recorder, and the Track Inspector.
5. Track Inspector: Before each trial, inspect the track to see that it is straight, the track pieces are flush, and the bells are hanging properly.
6. Starter: Set a marble 60 centimeters up the inclined track. When all group members are ready, let go of the marble and allow it to roll down the inclined track and onto the flat track.

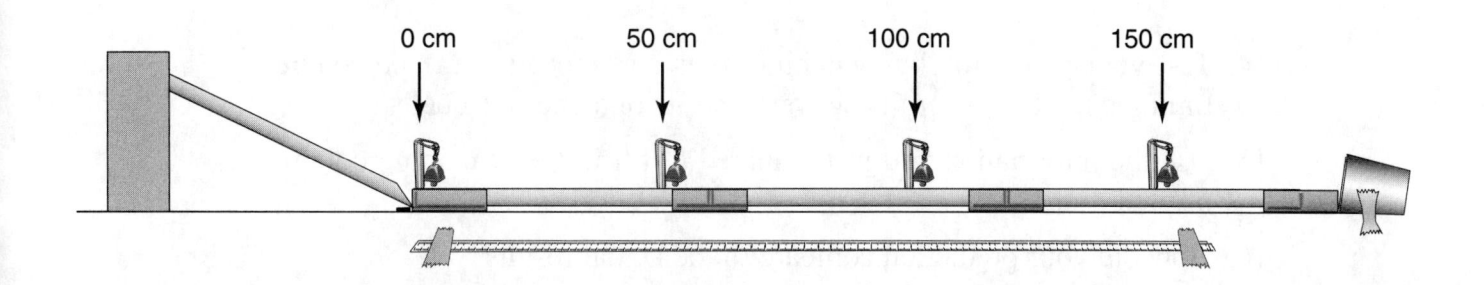

Figure 2: The flat track divided into three equal sections by the bell stands.

7. Timer: When the marble rings the first bell, start the stopwatch. When the marble rings the second bell, stop the stopwatch.
8. Recorder: Record the time in the chart below.

Time a Marble Takes to Roll Between Bells

	Time between Bells 1 and 2	Time between Bells 3 and 4	Time between Bells 2 and 3
Trial 1			
Trial 2			
Trial 3			
Average			

9. Repeat steps 5 through 8 two more times until your group has recorded three times in the chart.
10. Share the data from the Recorder's chart. Find the average of the three times and compare your answers. Enter the average in your chart.
11. Switch roles and repeat the procedure, but instead of timing a marble as it rolls between the first and second bells, time a marble as it rolls between the third and fourth bells.
12. Use the information in your chart to fill in the first and last columns of the graph on page 65.
13. How long do you predict it will take a marble to roll from Bell 2 to Bell 3?

___

14. Test your prediction by switching roles and repeating the procedure, timing a marble as it rolls between the second and third bells.
15. Use the information you just gathered to fill in the remaining column of your graph.
16. How did your prediction compare to the actual results?

___

___

Speeding Up or Slowing Down Bar Graph

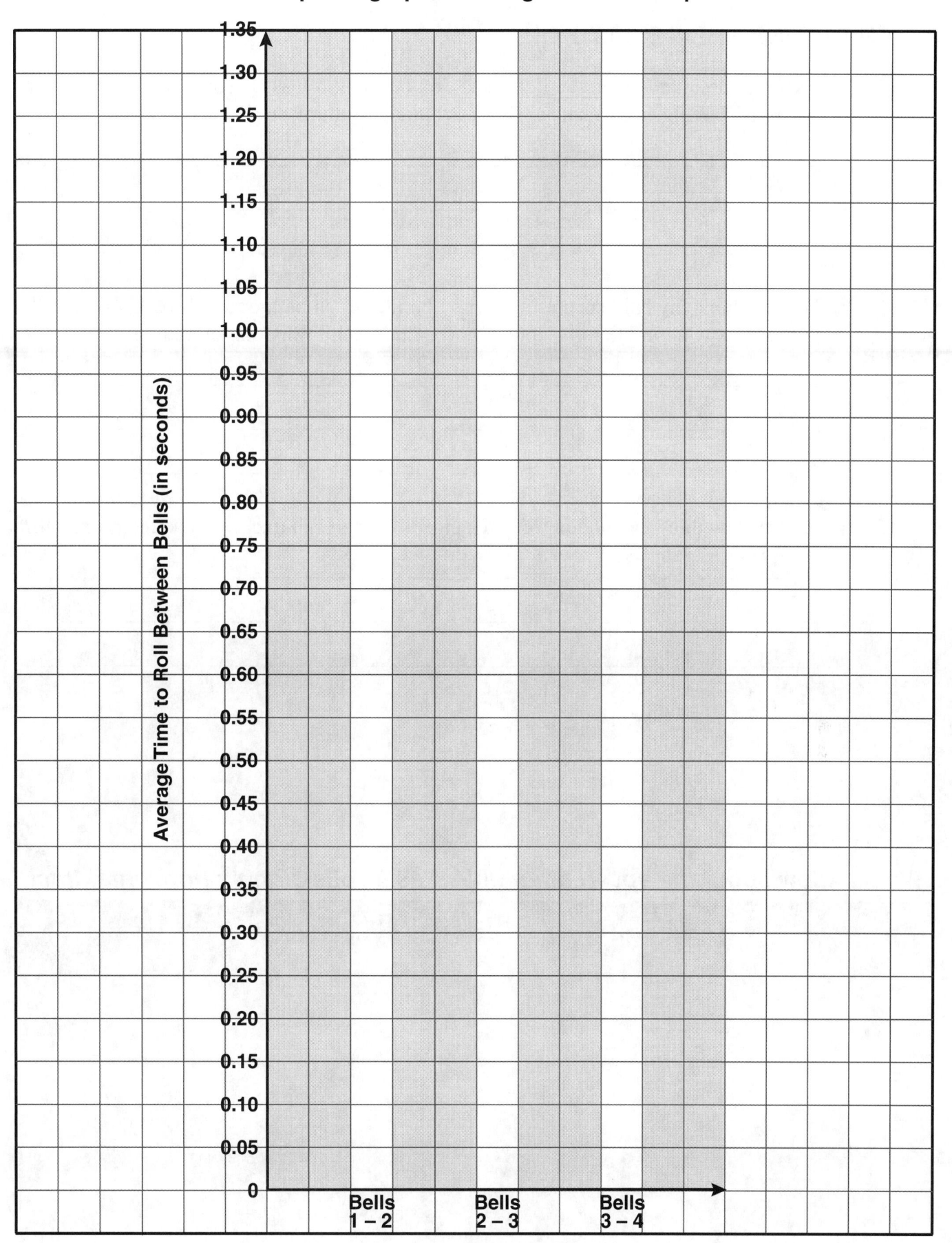

Average Time to Roll Between Bells (in seconds)

1.35
1.30
1.25
1.20
1.15
1.10
1.05
1.00
0.95
0.90
0.85
0.80
0.75
0.70
0.65
0.60
0.55
0.50
0.45
0.40
0.35
0.30
0.25
0.20
0.15
0.10
0.05
0

Bells 1–2   Bells 2–3   Bells 3–4

Section of Track

INTERPRETING THE RESULTS

? 1. As a marble rolled along the flat track, do you think it was speeding up, slowing down, or moving at a constant speed? Why do you think so?

_____

_____

_____

? 2. Do you think any ball, such as a bowling ball, a beach ball, or a golf ball, would roll the same way a marble rolls along a horizontal track? Why do you think so?

_____

_____

_____

? 3. How do you think the motion would change if the ball and track were perfectly smooth?

_____

_____

_____

What I know about the speed of an object as it rolls along a horizontal track

_____

_____

_____

_____

Exploration 12: Rolling Speed on an Inclined Track

RECORDING YOUR IDEAS

? 1. When a marble rolls down the inclined part of the track, do you think it is speeding up, slowing down, or moving at a constant speed? (See Figure 1.)

_____

_____

_____

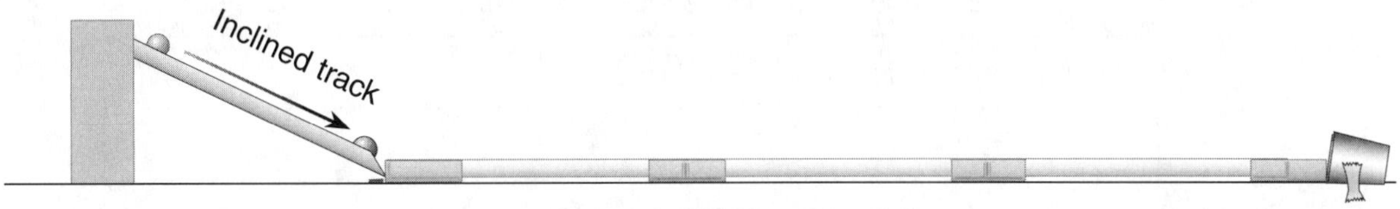

Figure 1: The marble rolling down the inclined track.

? 2. Why do you think so?

_____

_____

_____

? 3. How could you test your prediction?

_____

_____

_____

? 4. My question about the speed of an object as it rolls down a slope is

_____

_____

_____

EXPLORATION 12 PROCEDURE

Gather the following materials with your group.

✔	Materials Checklist
	Scissors
	4 tracks (including a red-ended track)
	3 connectors
	Tape measure
	2 pieces of card stock or file folder, 21.5 centimeters x 28 centimeters (8½ inches x 11 inches)
	Paper cup
	Tissue
	6 plastic marbles of the same size
	3 bell stands and Track Tower from Exploration 11

Part 1: Building Bell Towers

Now build three Bell Towers to support the track.

1. Working with your group, cut out one set of the Bell Tower templates on pages 69 and 71.

2. Glue the Bell Tower templates onto the pieces of card stock or file folder.

3. Cut out the templates. Cut along the solid lines to create Flaps A and B.

4. For each Bell Tower, fold the template along the dotted lines. Crease the folds.

5. Arrange each template so that you have a box shape with four sides and two open ends. Tape Flap C over the side (see Figure 2).

6. Fold Flaps A and B inward and use a piece of masking tape to connect the two flaps in the center of the tower (see Figure 2).

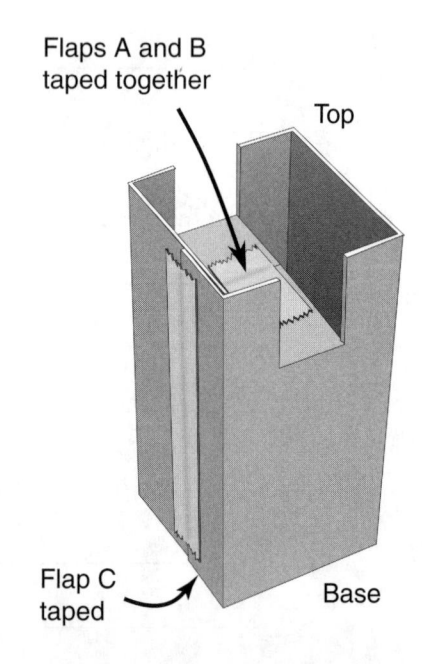

Figure 2: A Bell Tower.

Bell Tower 1 Template

Flap A

Flap B

Flap C

Back of Bell Tower 1 Template

Bell Tower 2 Template

Flap C
Flap B
Flap A
Flap C

Bell Tower 3 Template

Flap C
Flap B
Flap A
Flap C

Back of Bell Tower 3 Template

Back of Bell Tower 2 Template

Part 2: Setting Up an Inclined Track

Now set up the track so a marble will roll across three equal-length sections:

- Track Tower to Bell Tower 1
- Bell Tower 1 to Bell Tower 2
- Bell Tower 2 to Bell Tower 3

1. Use three connectors to attach all four track pieces together to make a long track with one red end.
2. Prop the end of the track that is not red on the Track Tower.
3. Use Bell Tower 1 to support the track at the highest connector. Put Bell Tower 2 at the middle connector. Put Bell Tower 3 at the lowest connector. The track should fit snugly into the rectangular cutouts of each Bell Tower (see Figure 3).
4. Place a tissue in the paper cup. Put the cup next to the red end at the bottom of the inclined track. Tape the cup to the work surface.
5. Start a marble at the very top of the track. Adjust the track if necessary to make the marble roll smoothly.

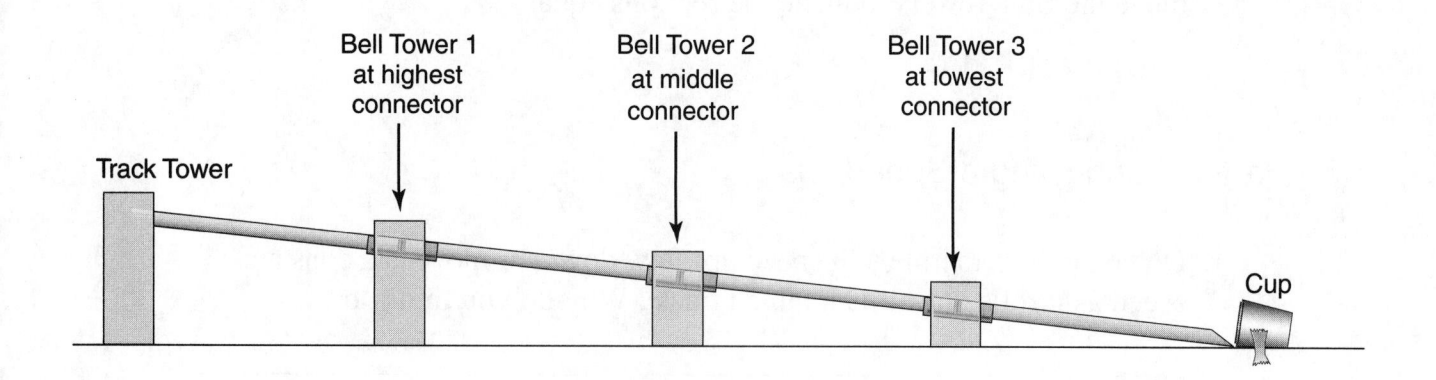

Figure 3: The towers supporting the track.

Part 3: Adding the Bells

1. Disassemble each bell stand by pulling the bottom paper clip (without a bell attached) out of the straw. Set aside this paper clip.

2. Hold the straw vertically against the side of one of the Bell Towers, so that the top of the straw is flush with the top edge of the Bell Tower (see Figure 4). Tape the straw in this position.

3. Position the paper clip so the bell hangs directly over the track (see Figure 4).

4. Add a bell to each of the other Bell Towers, but not to the Track Tower.

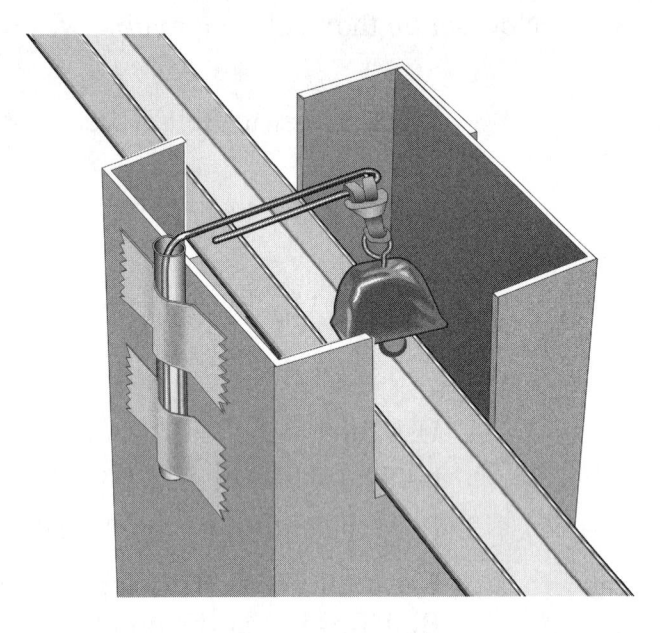

Figure 4: The bell hanging over the track.

5. Roll a marble down the track. Adjust each bell so it rings when the marble hits it. You can adjust a bell by moving the rubber band along the paper clip or by sliding the paper clip up or down in the straw.

6. Measure the length of the sections of track between the very top and the first bell, between the first bell and the second bell, and between the second bell and the third bell. If the sections are not equal in length, move the Bell Towers to make the sections equal.

Part 4: Conducting a Speed Trial

1. Do you think a marble will speed up, slow down, or move at a constant speed as it rolls down the inclined track? Why do you think so?

_____
_____
_____

2. Design a method to test whether a marble speeds up, slows down, or moves at a constant speed as it rolls down the inclined track. Answer the following questions to help you design your method:

   a) What can you measure to test whether a marble is speeding up, slowing down, or moving at a constant speed as it rolls down the incline?

   _____
   _____
   _____

   b) How can you use the apparatus to help you make these measurements?

   _____
   _____
   _____

   c) What will be the role of each group member?

   _____
   _____
   _____

   d) How can you check on the accuracy of your data?

   _____
   _____

   e) How many trials will you make? _____

   f) How will you record your results?

   _____
   _____
   _____

3. Ask your teacher to check your design and approve it.

4. Collect the materials you need and conduct your speed trials. Use the space below to record your data.

5. Use the data to make a graph on page 77. Answer the following questions to help you design your graph:

   a) How many columns will your graph have? Why?

   _____

   b) What labels will you place on the different columns?

   _____

   c) How will you know how high to make each column?

   _____

   _____

   d) What title would be a good description for the information in your graph?

   _____

6. What did you discover? _____

   _____

   _____

   _____

   _____

Title:

INTERPRETING THE RESULTS

? 1. Why do you think a marble keeps rolling down the inclined track?

_____

_____

? 2. What did this exploration show you about objects rolling down an incline?

_____

_____

? 3. How is the motion of a ball rolling down an inclined track different from the motion of a ball rolling along a flat track?

_____

_____

_____

? 4. How do you think the motion of an object that you drop compares with the motion of a ball rolling down an inclined track?

_____

_____

_____

***What I know about how the speed of an object changes
as it rolls down an incline***

_____

_____

_____

_____

_____

Unit 4: ACCELERATION AND THE ARIES SPEEDCART

Exploration 13: Building the Speedcart

RECORDING YOUR IDEAS

1. List the different kinds of four-wheeled vehicles you have seen.

2. What do you think makes each vehicle move?

3. Assume each of the vehicles is standing still. Do you think any one of them could start moving by itself? If so, how?

4. My question about rolling speed is

FORCE FIELDS

How fast is the Earth orbiting the Sun? The Earth's average speed as it orbits the Sun is about 30 kilometers per second (nearly 20 miles per second). In one day, the Earth travels about 2.6 million kilometers (1.6 million miles).

EXPLORATION 13 PROCEDURE

Part 1: Building the Speedcart

Collect the following materials with your group.

✔	Materials Checklist
	Piece of corrugated cardboard, 16 centimeters x 4.5 centimeters (about 6 ¼ inches x 1 ¾ inches)
	Metric ruler
	Scissors
	Plastic drinking straw
	4 rubber bands
	2 wooden dowels, each 8 centimeters (3 ⅛ inches long)
	4 plastic wheels (tires and hubs)
	4 small metal washers

1. Cut out the Speedcart template on page 81 and glue it onto the cardboard.

2. The template is marked with a 0.5 centimeter grid. That means each square of the grid measures 0.5 centimeters on a side.

    Measure 3 centimeters (6 squares) from one of the narrow ends of the cardboard. At this point, draw a line across the cardboard (see Figure 1).

3. From the opposite narrow end, measure 4 centimeters (8 squares). At this point, draw a line across the cardboard (see Figure 1). This line, and the line drawn in step 2, will be the *axle guide lines*.

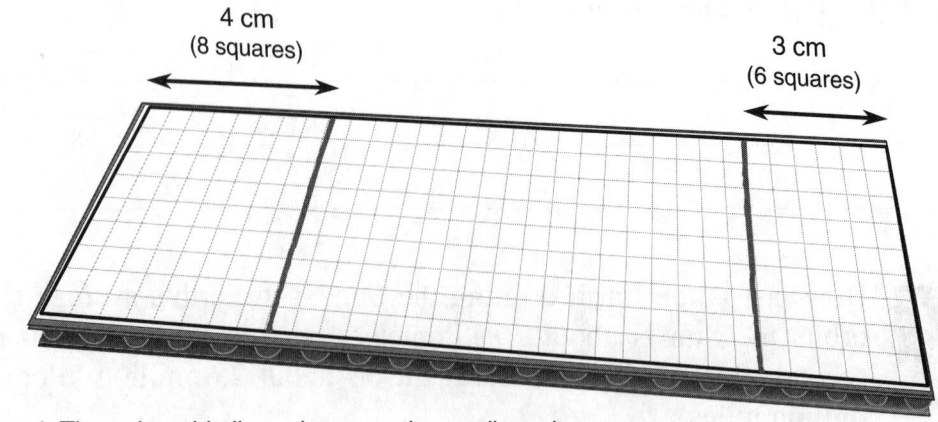

Figure 1: The axle guide lines drawn on the cardboard.

4. Measure and cut two 6 centimeter (2 ⅜ inch) pieces from the straw.

5. Hold one straw piece under the cardboard so it is directly under one of the axle guide lines. Position the straw so it extends an equal distance from each side of the cardboard (see Figure 2).

6. Secure the straw in this position with a rubber band. Loop the rubber band under one end of the straw. Pull the rubber band across the top of the cardboard and loop it under the other end of the straw (see Figure 2).

7. Use a second rubber band to keep the straw from sliding back and forth. Loop the second rubber band over one end of the straw. Pull the rubber band across the bottom of the cardboard and loop it over the other end of the straw (see Figure 3).

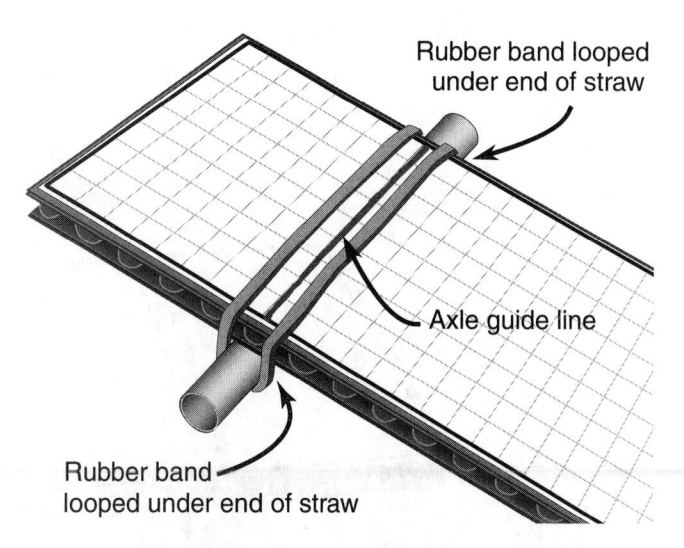

Figure 2: The straw held in place with one rubber band.

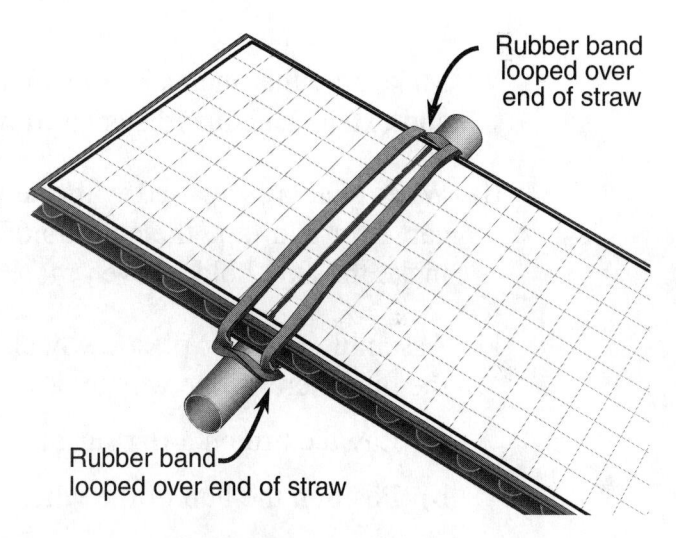

Figure 3: The straw held in place with two rubber bands.

Speedcart Template

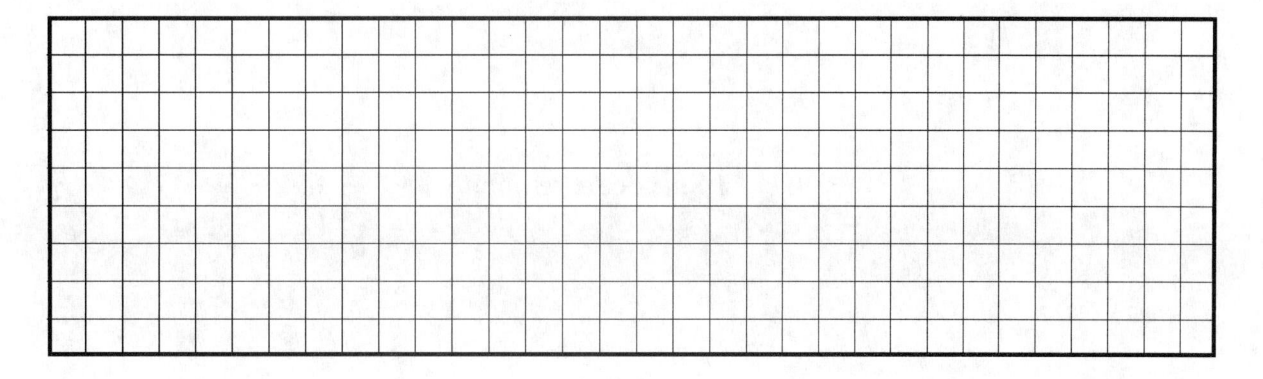

8. Attach the remaining straw piece under the second axle guide line using two rubber bands (see Figure 4). The two straw pieces are the *axle holders*.

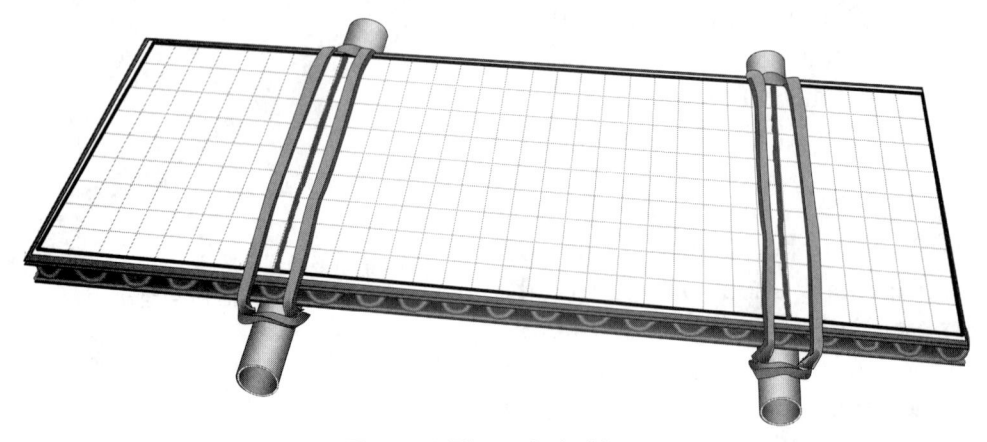

Figure 4: The axle holders.

9. Make sure that the axle holders are directly under the axle guide lines and extend an equal distance from each side of the cardboard.

10. When you are satisfied with the position of the axle holders, turn the cart over and tape the axle holders to the cardboard. This taping will make the axle holders even more stable.

11. Assemble the four plastic wheels. For each wheel, connect the tire to the hub. Here is one way to assemble a wheel:

    a) Lay the tire on a flat surface.

    b) Position the hub of the wheel directly over the tire.

    c) Push the hub down into the tire so that it snaps into place.

12. Each dowel will be the axle for one pair of wheels. Put one wheel on a dowel. Slide a metal washer onto the dowel from the other end as far as the wheel.

Back of Speedcart template

13. With the cart upside-down, slide the free end of the dowel through one of the axle holders (see Figure 5a).

14. Slide a second metal washer onto the dowel. Then push another wheel onto the free end of the dowel (see Figures 5a and 5b).

15. Assemble the remaining axle, wheels, and washers in the same way.

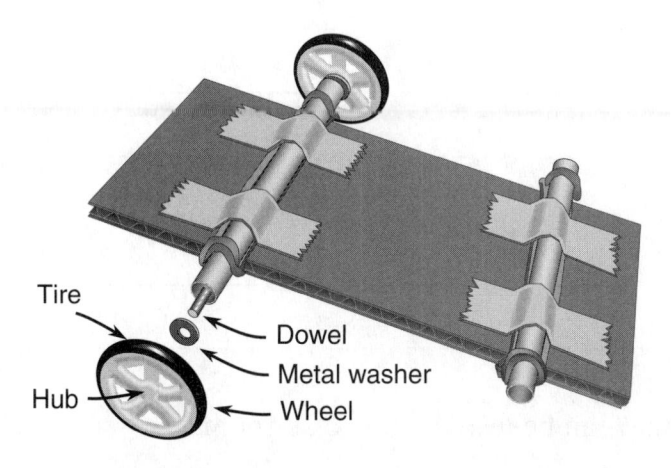

Figure 5a: One pair of wheels and washers attached with a dowel.

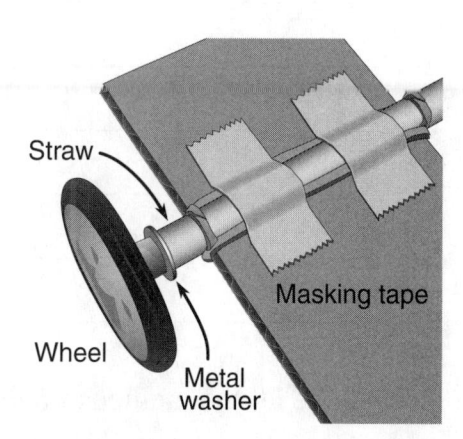

Figure 5b: Wheel, washer, and axle holder.

The Speedcart is now complete! Turn it over and give it a push. It should roll easily with all its wheels turning freely (see Figure 6).

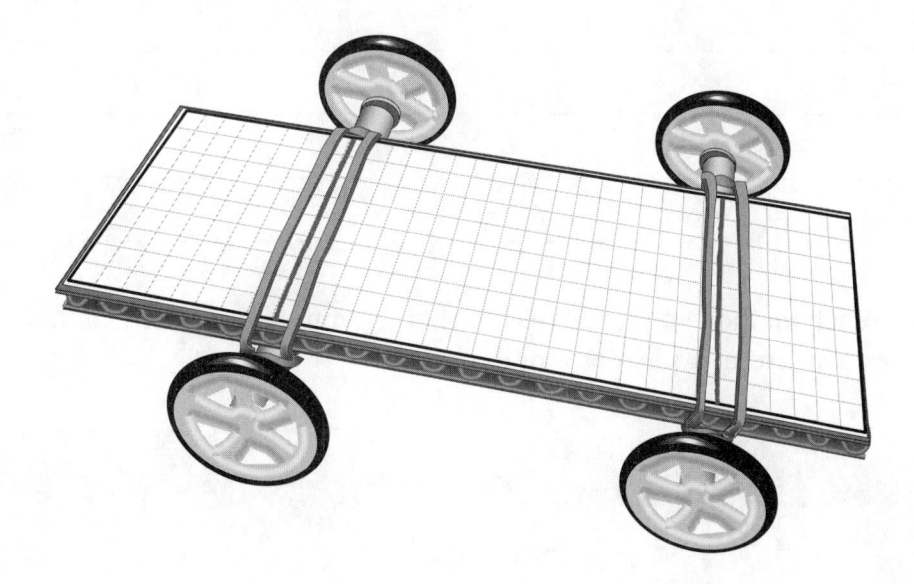

Figure 6: The completed Speedcart.

83

Part 2: Putting the Speedcart in Motion

The Speedcart can be used as a model for any wheeled vehicle — truck, car, train, or wagon. The investigations in this unit will help you to learn about the motion of all wheeled vehicles.

1. List different methods that you think would make your Speedcart start moving.

   _____
   _____
   _____
   _____
   _____
   _____

2. Circle all the methods in your list that can be tested in the classroom.

3. Test the different methods that you circled.

4. Based on your observations, which methods make your Speedcart start moving? List them.

   _____
   _____
   _____
   _____
   _____
   _____

5. Next to each method you listed, write whether you think the cart started to move because of a push or a pull.

INTERPRETING THE RESULTS

1. How is the motion of your Speedcart similar to the motion of an Air Disk?

_____

_____

_____

2. How is the motion of your Speedcart different from the motion of an Air Disk?

_____

_____

_____

3. Under what conditions would the motion of your Speedcart be similar to the motion of a marble rolling down an inclined track?

_____

_____

4. Under what conditions would the motion of your Speedcart be similar to the motion of a marble rolling along a flat track?

_____

_____

What I know about making a wheeled vehicle move

_____

_____

_____

_____

_____

Exploration 14: Powering the Speedcart

RECORDING YOUR IDEAS

With your group, tie a washer to one end of a 2.4 meter (about 8 foot) piece of string. Use the washer, string, and your Speedcart to answer the following questions.

? 1. Can you think of ways to get the Speedcart moving without actually pushing it with your hand? Make a list of methods you could try.

___

? 2. Where could the Speedcart be placed so it would start moving without the need for a push from you?

___

? 3. How could you use the washer and string to pull the Speedcart along a flat surface? Describe your method.

___

? 4. My question about Speedcart motion is

___

EXPLORATION 14 PROCEDURE

Collect the following materials with your group.

✔	Materials Checklist
	Speedcart
	Piece of string, 2.4 meters (about 8 feet) long
	Scissors
	Metric ruler
	2 large paper clips
	10 small washers in a cup
	Regular drinking straw
	Flexible drinking straw
	Drawing compass

Part 1: Assembling the Washer-Driven Cart

1. Write "Front" on the end of the cart that is 4 centimeters (8 squares) from the nearest axle. Write "Back" on the other end (see Figure 1).

2. Find the grid line that is 2 centimeters (4 squares) from the front end of the cart. Make a dot on the midpoint of the line (see Figure 1).

3. Use a drawing compass to make a hole through the dot (see Figure 1).

4. Bend each paper clip into an "S" shape, creating two hooks. Push one hook of one paper clip into the hole (see Figure 1).

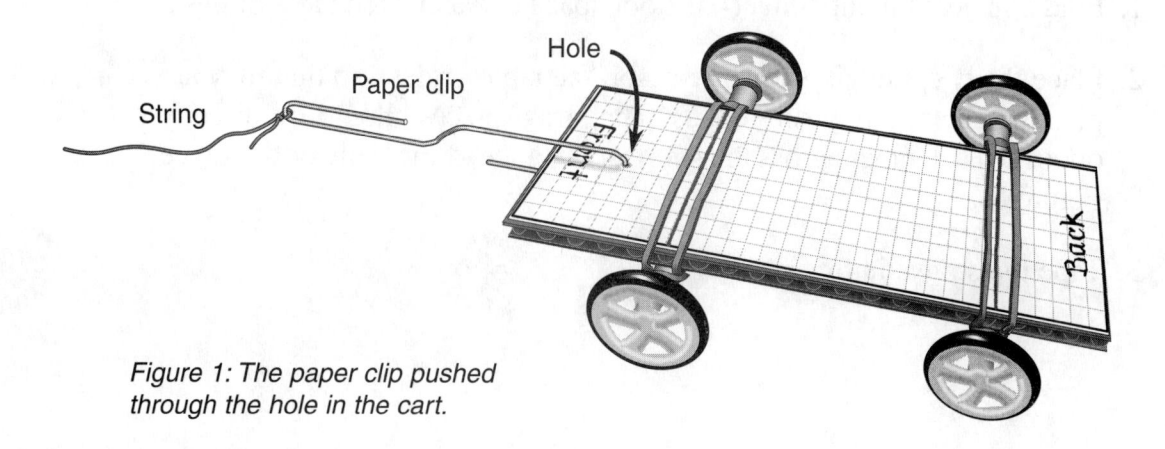

Figure 1: The paper clip pushed through the hole in the cart.

5. Tie one end of the string to the free hook of the paper clip. Tie at least two tight knots.

6. Find the midpoint of the flexible straw and cut it in half.

7. Slide the flexible half of the straw (the half with pleats) onto the free end of the string (see Figure 2). Set aside the other half of the straw.

8. Measure the regular drinking straw and cut it into two equal lengths.

9. Slide both portions of the regular drinking straw onto the free end of the string (see Figure 2).

10. Tie the free end of the string onto the smaller hook of the second paper clip (see Figure 2).

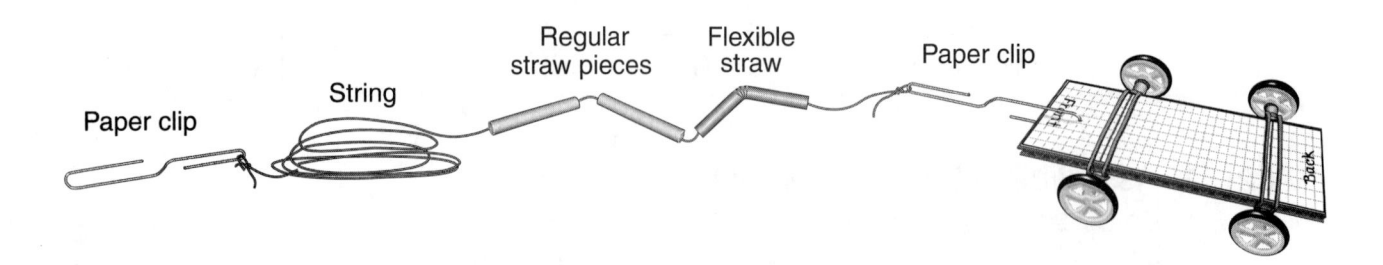

Figure 2: The straw pieces and paper clip attached to the string.

Part 2: Setting Up the Washer-Driven Cart

1. Find 3 meters (about 10 feet) of floor space and a cleared table or desk.

2. Place the two straight straw pieces on the table or desk so that they are perpendicular to opposite edges. The straw pieces should be directly opposite each other across the shortest distance of the table or desk (see Figure 3).

3. Tape the straws in this position.

Figure 3: The straws taped in place.

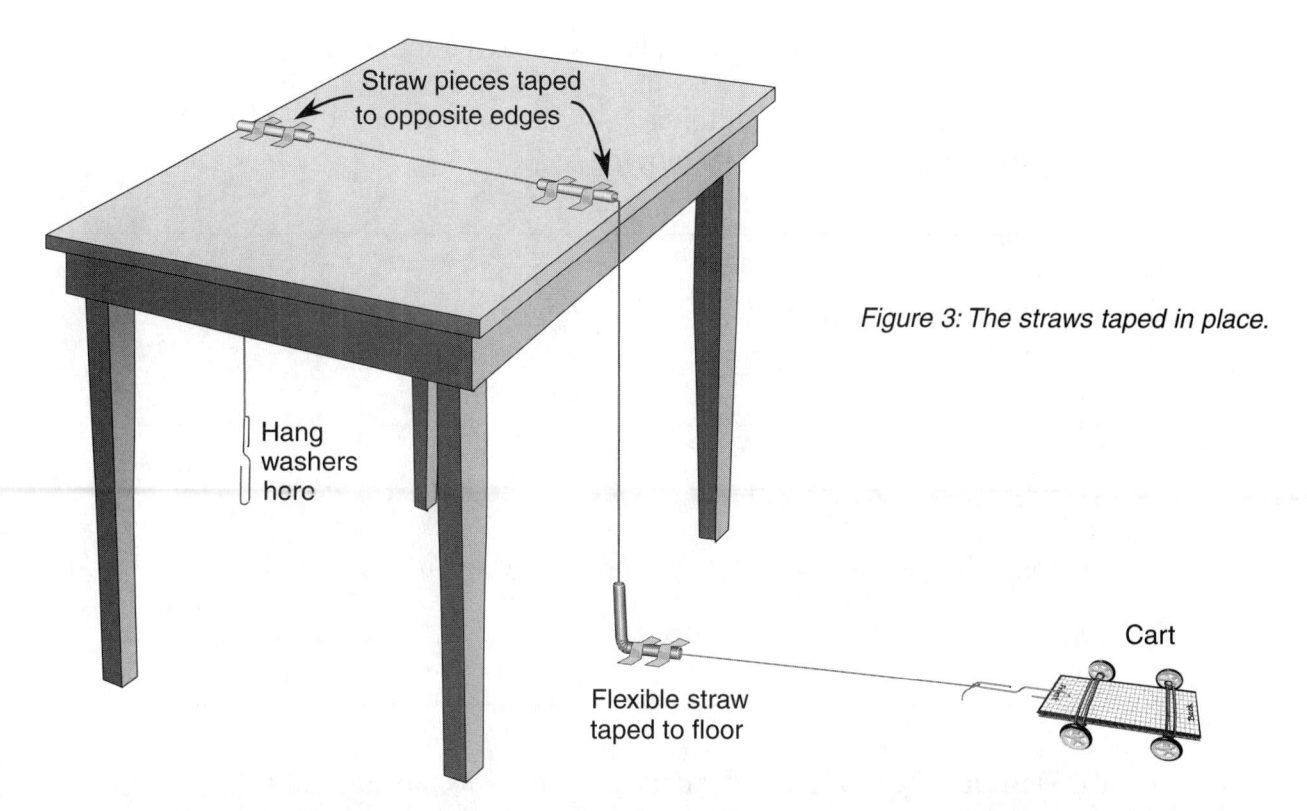

4. Bend the flexible drinking straw so it makes a right angle and set it on the floor, just below one of the straight straw pieces (see Figure 3).

5. Tape the straw to the floor in this position.

Part 3: Putting the Washer-Driven Cart in Motion

1. Decide which group members will be Cart Commanders and which will be Mass Masters.

2. Cart Commanders: Pull the cart along the floor, as far back from the table or desk as the string will allow. Hold the cart in this position.

3. Mass Masters: Hang washers from the bottom hook of the paper clip (see Figure 4).

4. Cart Commanders: When everyone is ready, release the cart.

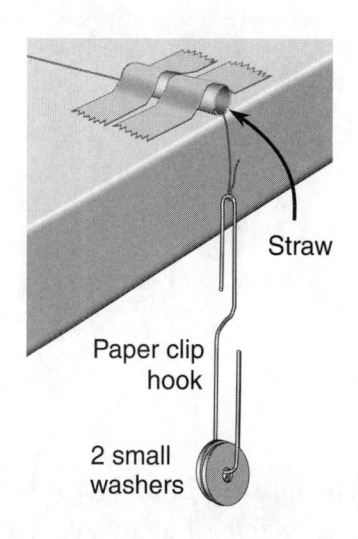

Figure 4: Washers hanging from the paper clip hook.

5. Use your washer-driven cart to find answers to the following questions:

   a) What is the minimum number of washers you need to add to the hook to make the cart start moving?
   _____

   b) What do you observe about the motion of the cart as you add more washers to the hook?
   _____
   _____

   c) Describe the motion of the cart *before* the washers fall.
   _____
   _____

   d) Describe the motion of the cart *while* the washers are falling.
   _____
   _____

   e) Describe the motion of the cart right after the washers have hit the ground.
   _____
   _____

FORCE FIELDS

The *mass* of an object is a measure of the amount of material in the object. The *weight* of an object is a measure of the gravitational forces acting on the object. For example, a large stone would have the same mass on Earth, Mars, and Jupiter; yet its weight would be different at each of the three sites.

INTERPRETING THE RESULTS

1. What makes a washer-driven cart start moving?

_____

_____

_____

2. Does the washer-driven cart move because of a push or a pull?

_____

3. How does adding more washers affect the motion of the cart?

_____

_____

4. What happens to the motion of the cart after the washers hit the ground?

_____

_____

5. If the string came untied, do you think the cart would keep going? Why or why not?

_____

_____

_____

What I know about the motion of a washer-driven cart

Exploration 15: Increasing the Falling Mass

RECORDING YOUR IDEAS

1. Think back to the washer-driven cart you used. What did you observe about the motion of the cart as you added more washers to the hook?

2. Describe why you think this happened.

3. Could you measure how each additional washer affects the cart's motion? If so, how?

4. My question about how mass affects motion is

EXPLORATION 15 PROCEDURE

Collect the following materials with your group. Each group will need one member who has a watch that can be used to time the trials to at least tenths of a second.

✔	Materials Checklist
	Washer-driven cart
	Tape measure
	8 small washers in a paper cup
	2 textbooks

Part 1: Building a Barricade

1. Working with your group, set up the washer-driven cart the same way you did before (see Figure 1).
2. Pull the cart along the floor, as far back from the table or desk as the string will allow.

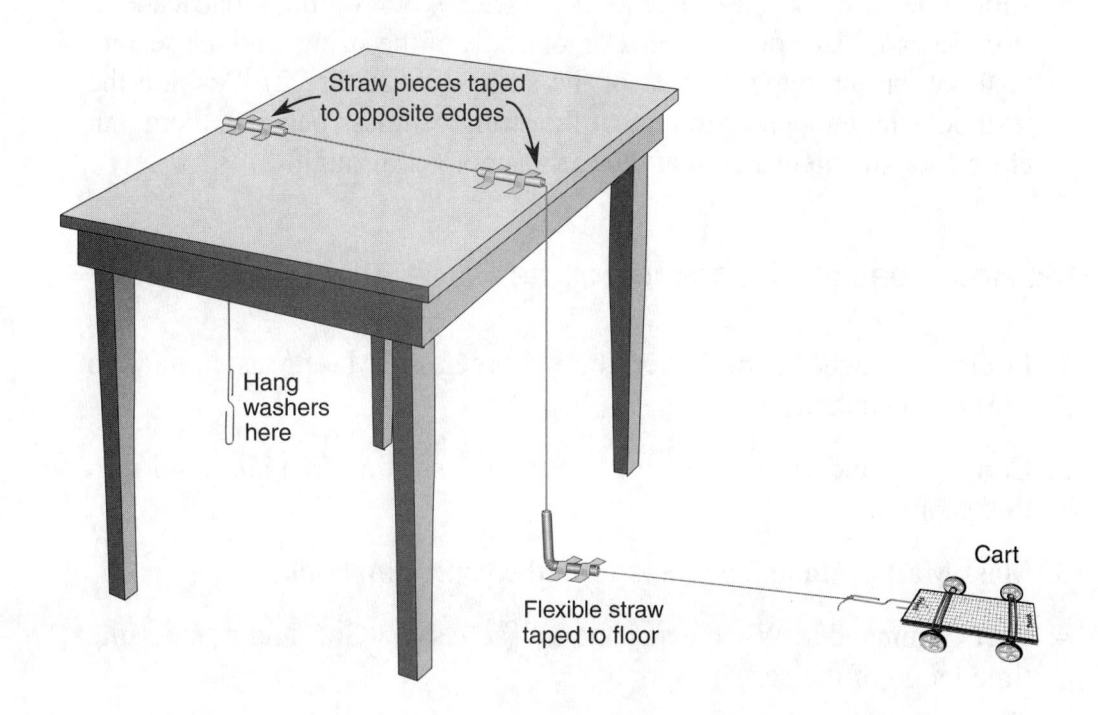

Figure 1: The washer-driven cart setup.

93

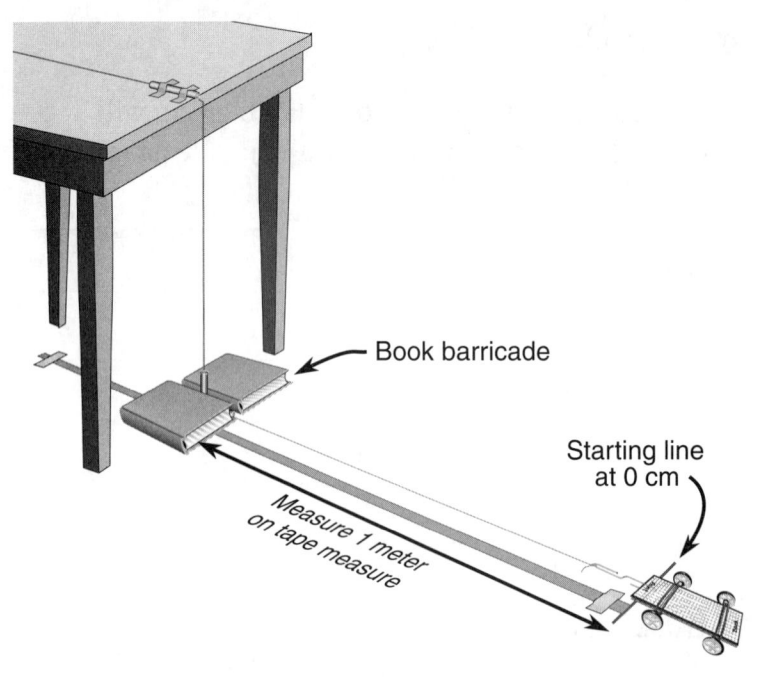

Figure 2: The barricade built 1 meter from the starting line.

3. While holding the cart in this position, stick a piece of masking tape to the floor just in front of the cart's front wheels (see Figure 2). The tape will serve as the starting line.

4. Position a tape measure (metric side up) between the cart and the table or desk so the 0 centimeter end is flush with the starting line (see Figure 2). Use masking tape to hold the tape measure parallel to the string.

5. Along the string at 1 meter (about 40 inches), build a book barricade to stop the cart. Place one textbook on one side of the string, and the second textbook on the opposite side of the string (see Figure 2). Position the textbooks far enough apart so that the string can pass between them, but close enough together so that the cart cannot get through.

Part 2: How Does the Magnitude of the Force Affect Cart Speed?

1. Decide who will be the Timer, the Recorder, the Mass Master, and the Cart Commander.

2. Cart Commander: Pull the cart back to the starting line and hold it in this position.

3. Mass Master: Hang 2 washers from the paper clip hook.

4. Cart Commander: When everyone is ready, say, "Go," and at the same time let go of the cart.
   Timer: When the Cart Commander says, "Go," start the stopwatch.

5. Timer: At the very moment the cart hits the barricade, stop the stopwatch.

6. Recorder: Record the time in the chart below.

7. Repeat steps 2 through 6 two more times until you have completed three trials.

8. Share the data from the Recorder's chart. Find the average of the three times and compare your answers. Write the average in your chart.

9. Switch roles and repeat the procedure with 4, 6, and 8 washers on the hook.

Number of Washers on Hook and Time

Number of washers on hook	Time (seconds)	Description of cart motion
2	Trial 1: Trial 2: Trial 3: Average:	
4	Trial 1: Trial 2: Trial 3: Average:	
6	Trial 1: Trial 2: Trial 3: Average:	
8	Trial 1: Trial 2: Trial 3: Average:	

Title: _____

10. After your group has completed all the trials, use the information you gathered to make a graph.

   Label the different columns.

   Write a title that explains the information in your graph.

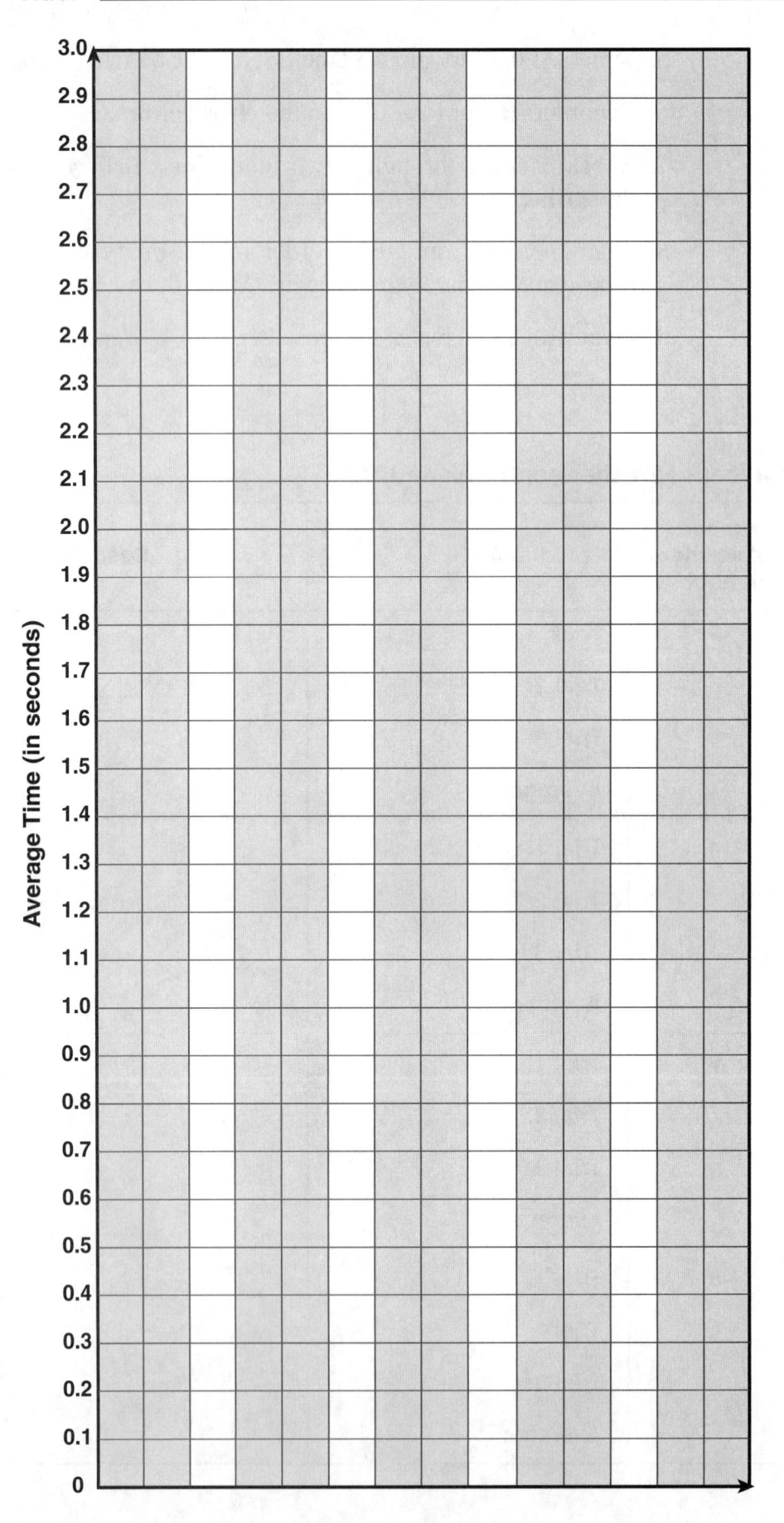

Average Time (in seconds)

3.0
2.9
2.8
2.7
2.6
2.5
2.4
2.3
2.2
2.1
2.0
1.9
1.8
1.7
1.6
1.5
1.4
1.3
1.2
1.1
1.0
0.9
0.8
0.7
0.6
0.5
0.4
0.3
0.2
0.1
0

INTERPRETING THE RESULTS

1. What did you observe about the motion of the cart as you added more washers to the hook?

2. Why do you think your cart behaved as it did?

What I know about how increasing the falling mass affects cart motion

Exploration 16: Adding Mass to the Cart

RECORDING YOUR IDEAS

? 1. Think about what happened in the last exploration when you added washers to the hook. How long did it take the cart to travel 1 meter when 6 washers were on the hook?

_____
_____
_____

? 2. With 6 washers on the hook, how could you make your cart go slower than it did?

_____
_____
_____

? 3. Do you think it is possible to make a cart with more mass move as fast as a cart with less mass? If so, what would you have to do?

_____
_____
_____

? 4. My question about how to make the cart move slower is

_____
_____
_____

EXPLORATION 16 PROCEDURE

Collect the following materials with your group. Each group will need one member who has a watch that can be used to time the trials to at least tenths of a second.

✔	Materials Checklist
	Washer-driven cart
	Tape measure
	6 small washers
	4 large washers
	Cup to hold washers
	2 textbooks
	Rubber band

1. Working with your group, set up your cart just as you did in the last exploration (see Figure 1).
2. Decide who will be the Timer, the Recorder, the Mass Master, and the Cart Commander.
3. Cart Commander: Pull the cart back to the starting line and hold the cart in this position.
4. Mass Master: Hang 6 SMALL washers from the paper clip hook.
5. Cart Commander: Use a rubber band to attach 1 LARGE washer to the top of the cart (see Figure 2).

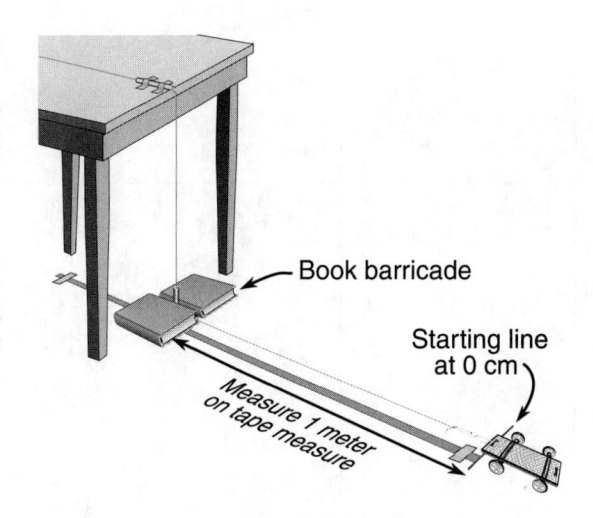

Figure 1: The washer-driven cart setup.

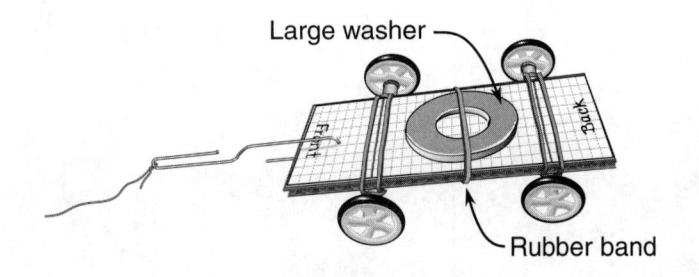

Figure 2: A large washer attached to the cart.

6. Cart Commander: When everyone is ready, say, "Go" and let go of the cart.
   Timer: When the Cart Commander says, "Go," start the stopwatch.
7. Timer: Stop the stopwatch at the moment the cart hits the barricade.
8. Recorder: Record the time in the chart below.
9. Repeat steps 3 through 8 two more times until your group has completed three trials.
10. Share the data from the Recorder's chart. Find the average of the times for the three trials and compare your answers. Write the average in your chart.
11. Switch roles and repeat the procedure, keeping the 6 small washers on the hook, but attaching 2, then 3, then 4 large washers to the top of the cart.

Number of Washers on Cart and Time

Number of large washers on cart	Time (seconds)	Description of cart motion
1	Trial 1: Trial 2: Trial 3: Average:	
2	Trial 1: Trial 2: Trial 3: Average:	
3	Trial 1: Trial 2: Trial 3: Average:	
4	Trial 1: Trial 2: Trial 3: Average:	

Title: _____

12. After you have completed all the trials, use the data to make a graph.

    Label the different columns.

    Add a title that explains the information in your graph.

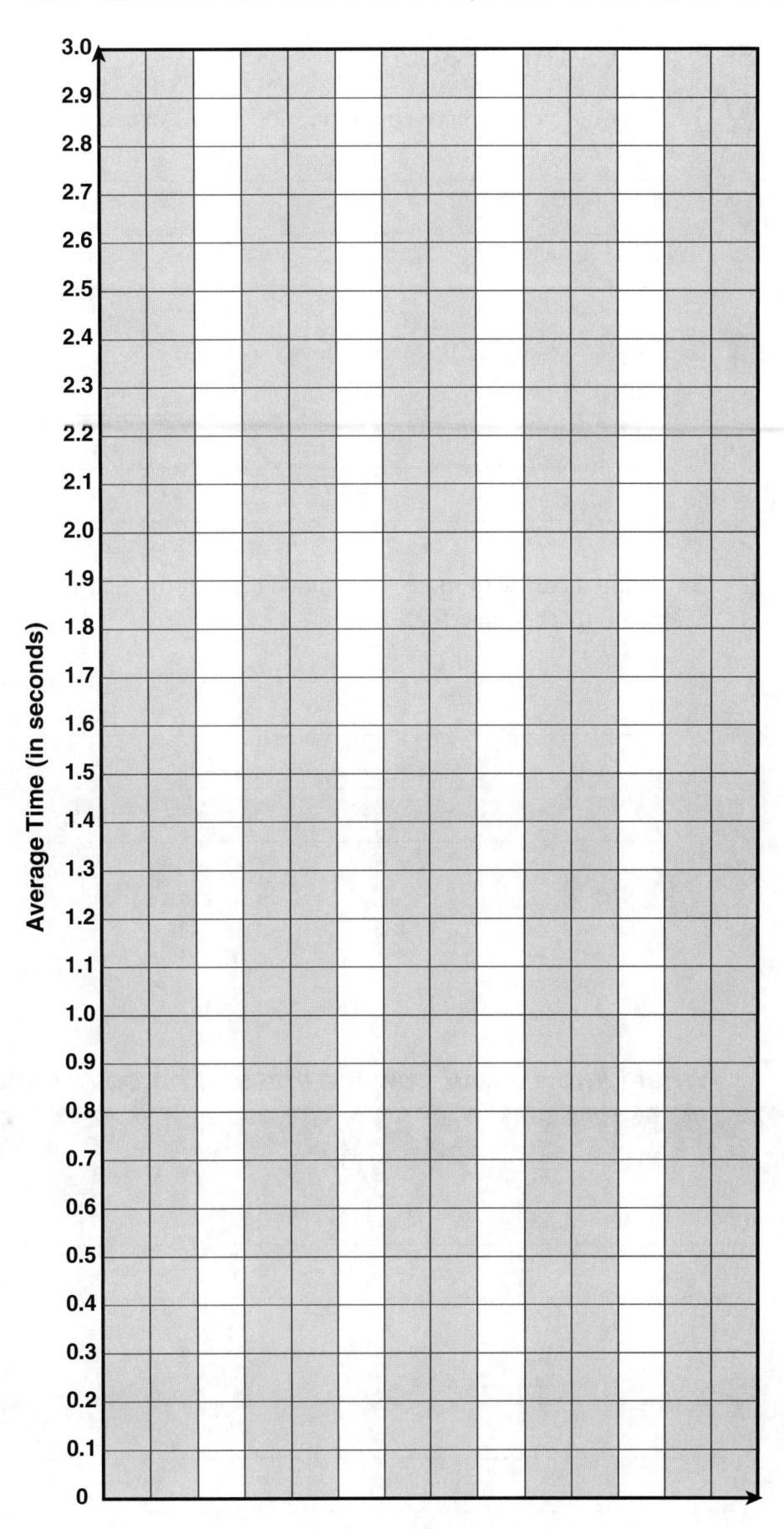

Average Time (in seconds): 0, 0.1, 0.2, 0.3, 0.4, 0.5, 0.6, 0.7, 0.8, 0.9, 1.0, 1.1, 1.2, 1.3, 1.4, 1.5, 1.6, 1.7, 1.8, 1.9, 2.0, 2.1, 2.2, 2.3, 2.4, 2.5, 2.6, 2.7, 2.8, 2.9, 3.0

INTERPRETING THE RESULTS

1. What did you observe about the motion of the cart as more washers were added to it?

_____
_____
_____

2. Why do you think the cart behaved as it did?

_____
_____
_____

3. Would a cart with more mass move differently than a cart with less mass if each were pulled by the same force?

_____
_____
_____
_____

What I know about how the mass of an object affects its motion

_____
_____
_____
_____
_____

Exploration 17: A Fan-Powered Speedcart

RECORDING YOUR IDEAS

? 1. How does the turning propeller on a boat make the boat move?

_____
_____
_____
_____

? 2. How could you use a fan (a propeller attached to a motor) to make your cart move? List as many ways as you can.

_____
_____
_____
_____
_____

? 3. My question about a fan cart is

_____
_____
_____

FORCE FIELDS Fan-driven boats are often associated with the Florida Everglades swamp. In reality, though, they are not allowed in the Everglades National Park. The noise the boats produce and the paths they make through the vegetation pose too great a danger to the environment.

103

EXPLORATION 17 PROCEDURE

Collect the following materials with your group.

✔	Materials Checklist
	Speedcart
	Polystyrene foam block, 4.5 cm x 3.8 cm x 3.8 cm (about 1 ¾ in x 1 ½ in x 1 ½ in)
	2 small rubber bands
	Metric ruler
	Motor with 2 wire test leads
	AA battery
	AA battery holder
	Propeller
	Large rubber band

1. Position the foam block on the front of the cart so a 4.5 centimeter (about 1 ¾ inch) edge is aligned along the front edge of the cart (see Figure 1).

2. Use the two small rubber bands to hold the foam block to the cart (see Figure 1). The foam block will be the motor mount of your fan cart.

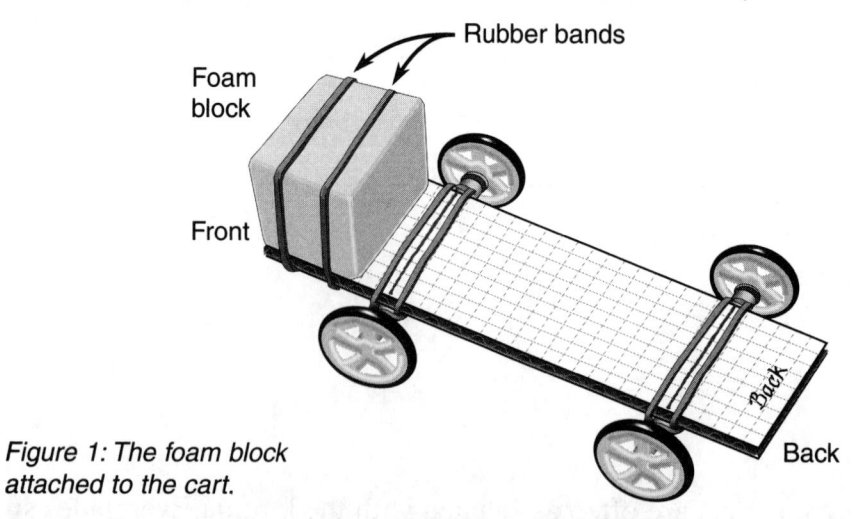

Figure 1: The foam block attached to the cart.

! The fan will not hurt you if you touch the spinning blade while it is turning, but the motor may be damaged if you stop it this way.

3. Position the motor on the foam block with the propeller shaft extending past the front of the foam block (see Figure 2).

4. Wrap the large rubber band around the motor, the foam block, and the cart base (see Figure 2).

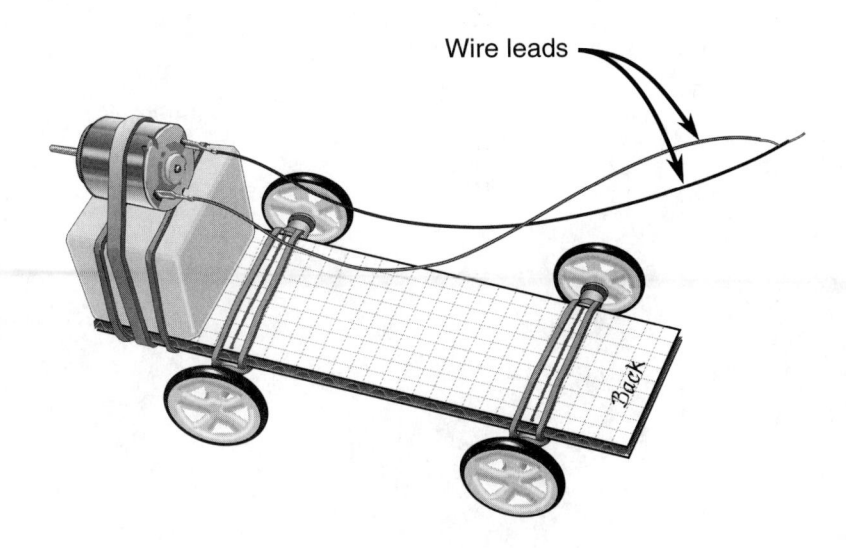

Figure 2: The motor attached to the cart.

5. Put the battery into the battery holder.

6. Place the battery holder on the back of the cart (see Figure 3). Use the grid to help you center the battery holder along the width of the cart.

   Tape the battery holder to the cart (see Figure 3). Make sure the tape does not interfere with the spin of the back axle.

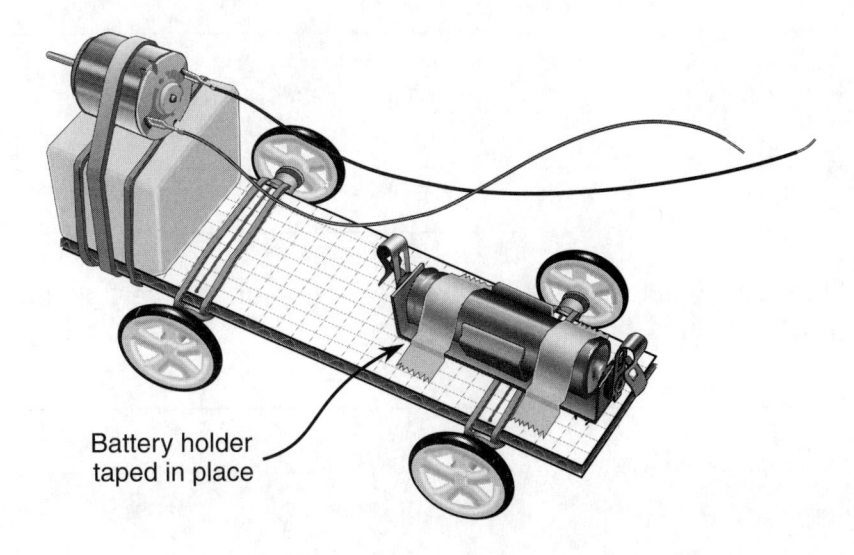

Figure 3: The battery holder added to the cart.

7. Push the propeller onto the propeller shaft. Spin the propeller with your finger. It should spin freely without hitting the cart or the foam block (see Figure 4).

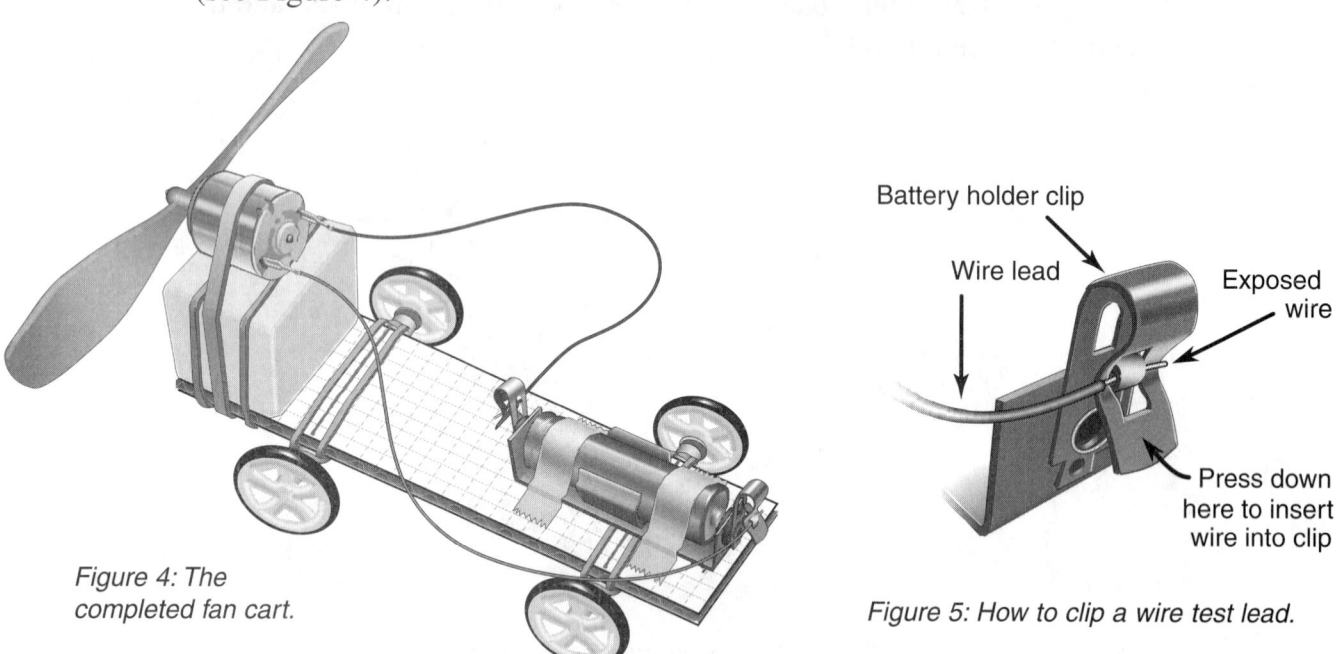

Figure 4: The completed fan cart.

Figure 5: How to clip a wire test lead.

8. Insert the wire test leads into the clips on the battery holder (see Figures 4 and 5). Set the fan cart down and watch it move!

9. Investigate the motion of the fan cart by finding answers to the following questions:

   a) How can you make your fan cart move forward?

   _____
   _____

   b) How can you make your fan cart move backward?

   _____
   _____

   c) How can you change the direction of your fan cart while it is moving?

   _____
   _____

INTERPRETING THE RESULTS

1. What do you think makes the fan cart move? What evidence supports your answer?

_____

_____

2. Describe how the motion of the fan cart changes with time.

_____

_____

3. If the propeller stopped turning, would the fan cart continue to move?

_____

_____

4. If you had enough space, would the fan cart keep going? Why or why not?

_____

_____

_____

What I know about fan cart motion

_____

_____

_____

_____

_____

Exploration 18: How Fast Can the Fan Cart Move?

RECORDING YOUR IDEAS

? 1. Describe the motion of your fan cart.

_____
_____
_____

? 2. As the fan cart moves, do you think it speeds up, slows down, or moves at a constant speed?

_____
_____
_____

? 3. What are some strategies you might use to determine if the fan cart is speeding up, slowing down, or moving at a constant speed?

_____
_____
_____

? 4. My question about fan cart motion is

_____
_____
_____

FORCE FIELDS The planet Mercury was named after the character in Greek mythology who was a winged messenger of the heavens. This name is appropriate because Mercury moves faster than any other planet in the solar system. It orbits the Sun in about 88 days, traveling about 170,000 kilometers per hour (nearly 110,000 miles per hour), on average. By contrast, the Earth travels about 106,000 kilometers per hour (about 67,000 miles per hour) on average, and Pluto about 17,000 kilometers per hour (nearly 11,000 miles per hour).

EXPLORATION 18 PROCEDURE

Collect the following materials with your group. Each group will need one member who has a watch that can be used to time the trials to at least tenths of a second.

✔	Materials Checklist
	Fan cart
	Tape measure

1. Design a method to determine if the fan cart speeds up, slows down, or moves at a constant speed. Answer the following questions to help guide your plan.

   a) How can you make your fan cart move in a straight line?

   _____

   b) Why is it important that the fan cart move in a straight line?

   _____

   c) What will you measure to determine if the fan cart is speeding up, slowing down, or moving at a constant speed?

   _____

   _____

   d) Into how many sections will you divide the distance? _____

   e) How many trials will you do? _____

   f) How will you determine the precise moment to begin and end timing each trial?

   _____

   _____

   g) What responsibilities will each group member have?

   _____

   _____

2. Write a list of steps with a diagram to show your method.

3. Ask your teacher to check your method and approve it.

4. With your group, try out your method. Use Table 1: Average Time for Each Section to record the times for each trial. Use column A to record results for the first section of the distance and add or cross out other columns to match your plan. You can make a larger table if your method calls for more than three trials.

5. Add the trial times you wrote in column A. Record the total in column A. Divide the total time by the number of trials to find the average time. Record it in column A. Now calculate the average time for each of the other sections of the distance.

Table 1: Average Time for Each Section

	A.		
Trial 1 time			
Trial 2 time			
Trial 3 time			
Total time			
Total time ÷ number of trials = Average time			

6. Now use Table 2 to calculate the average speed of the fan cart as it moved along each section:

   a) Write in column A the distance the cart traveled across the first section.

   b) Write the average time from Table 1 for the first section.

   c) Divide the distance by the average time to get the average speed for the section. Write the average speed the cart went as it crossed the first section.

   d) Now calculate the average speed for each of the other sections. Make a larger table with more columns if you need them.

Table 2: Average Speed for Each Section

	A.		
Distance			
Average time (from Table 1)			
Distance ÷ average time = Average speed			

7. On page 112, create a graph to display the average speed data. Answer the following questions to help plan your graph:

   a) What should the title of your graph be?

   _____

   b) If you wanted to show how the speed changes as the cart continues to move, what would you label the coordinates of your graph?

   _____

   c) Do you think the speed will keep on increasing as the cart moves along?

   _____

Title: _____

INTERPRETING THE RESULTS

1. Look at your graph. What does it tell you about the fan cart's motion?

_____

_____

_____

2. In what way is the motion of the fan cart similar to that of a ball rolling down an inclined track?

_____

_____

_____

3. What do we mean when we say, "The fan cart accelerates"?

_____

_____

_____

4. How is the motion of the fan cart similar to that of a real car?

_____

_____

_____

What I know about acceleration

_____

_____

_____

_____

_____

KEEP ON MOVING

Motion is a fascinating subject when you stop to think about it! Astronomers have been thinking about motion for centuries. Perhaps that's why they first wondered what made some things stay up and other things fall down; what made some things stay put and other things move in all sorts of different ways.

Many famous scientists such as Galileo, Newton, and Einstein observed and investigated the way things fall, roll, drop, soar, and orbit. The story of the apple falling on Newton's head may or may not be true, but Newton's observations of objects falling to the Earth and the motion of the Moon led to the formulation of his model of gravity.

Did you ever throw a baseball right by a hitter, write your name on smooth paper, jump over a puddle after a rainstorm, or open a stuck locker door? If so, in each case you used pushes and pulls to create just the right force to give the motion you needed.

You have studied speed, friction, and acceleration in this module. We hope you will go on to use what you learned in many different ways: in your home, on the sports field, and perhaps in your career. There may even come a time when your understanding of motion and forces can help you be one of the "movers and shakers" of your time.